# KENTUCKY
## AND THE WAR OF 1812

# KENTUCKY
## AND THE WAR OF 1812

The Governor, the Farmers and the Pig

DORIS DEAREN SETTLES

THE
History
PRESS

Published by The History Press
Charleston, SC
www.historypress.com

*Frontispiece*: The governor, a Kaintuck and a pig. *Drawn by Karen Loeffler, 2023.*

First published 2023

Manufactured in the United States

ISBN 9781467154857

Library of Congress Control Number: 2023934843

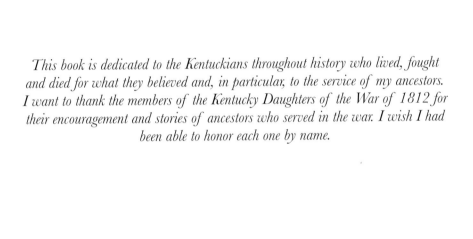

*This book is dedicated to the Kentuckians throughout history who lived, fought and died for what they believed and, in particular, to the service of my ancestors. I want to thank the members of the Kentucky Daughters of the War of 1812 for their encouragement and stories of ancestors who served in the war. I wish I had been able to honor each one by name.*

# CONTENTS

Preface                                                          9

1. War of 1812 Timeline                                         11
2. A New Nation                                                 16
3. Kentucky Before 1812                                         26
4. Isaac Shelby, the Governor                                   48
5. Henry Clay and the War Hawks                                 55
6. Tecumseh and Tenskwatawa                                     70
7. Women and Slaves in the War of 1812                          85
8. Remember the Raisin!                                         95
9. Kentucky Militia—and Pig—Response                           104
10. The Treaty of Ghent and Other Outcomes                     119
11. Notable Kentuckians in the War of 1812                     126
12. Kentucky Today                                             138

Sources and Further Reading                                    151
Index                                                          155
About the Author                                               159

# PREFACE

I love history, in all its messiness and offensiveness. We are people of our times, and we have learned much from our predecessors. What was the norm in 1811–13, in many instances, would be inappropriate today. The major players in this historical period—Native Americans, fledgling Americans and the British—all had a part to play. Sometimes one of them was more honorable than another; in another moment, it was another player who was kind, honorable, ethical. Tecumseh held himself and others to high ethical standards, but he encouraged killing to defend his people and land. The Kentucky militiamen, including Governor Shelby, killed to protect their families but mainly were peace-loving farmers. The British armies and sympathizers were also protecting land and income they felt was their right after losing much during the American Revolution. None of us is perfect, even after two hundred years. I have tried to write this book with sympathy for all sides but align the events with the historical moment in which they occurred. I ask you to do the same and see if the lessons from history might inform how you live your life today.

Chapter 1

# WAR OF 1812 TIMELINE

T he War of 1812 was primarily fought on two fronts: the East Coast and the Northwest Territories. Unfortunately, history has sidelined the experiences and effects of this war for whatever reason, and we are the poorer for it. This book focuses on the large part Kentucky and Kentuckians had in instigating, fighting and winning the War of 1812. While not a single battle or skirmish took place on Kentucky soil, "Kaintucks"—as they were known—were actively involved from beginning to end. This is the story of one of the most significant events in Kentucky and, for my two cents, United States history.

This basic timeline focuses primarily on the events that took place on the Northwest Territory front but includes a few significant events that occurred elsewhere for full context.

## 1811

| November 11 | The Battle of Tippecanoe sets the stage for the War of 1812. |

## 1812

| April 30 | Louisiana admitted to the Union. |
| June 18 | President Madison signs the Declaration of War. |

| July 12 | American general William Hull invades Canada from Detroit. |
| July 17 | Fort Michilimackinac surrenders to British-Canadian forces. |
| August 13 | General Hull surrenders Detroit to British-Canadian-Indigenous forces. |
| August 19 | USS *Constitution* takes HMS *Guerriere*. |
| December 28 | William Henry Harrison formally resigns as governor of Indiana Territory and takes the rank of brigadier general over all northwest armies. |

## 1813

| January 22 | The Battle of River Raisin: 100 percent of American combatants are Kentuckians; roughly five hundred of those are missing, killed or injured, including forty to sixty Kentucky captured soldiers who are brutally massacred, prompting the battle cry "Remember the Raisin." |
| March 4 | James Madison is sworn in for his second term as president. |
| March 27 | American commodore Oliver Hazard Perry takes command of the flotilla at British-controlled Lake Erie. |
| April 27 | York (present-day Toronto) is captured by Americans. Zebulon Pike is killed. |
| April 28–May 9 | American major general William Henry Harrison and his men hold Fort Meigs in the face of two consecutive British sieges. |
| May 5 | Dudley's Defeat: During the siege at Fort Meigs, Colonel William Dudley attacks the British at dawn successfully. The raw recruits, exhilarated by success, pursue straggling Native Americans into the forest, where they are killed and captured. Tecumseh stops the slaughter and chastises the Natives. |

| | |
|---|---|
| June 1 | Plans begin to take shape to invade Lower Canada and secure the city of Montreal in order to cut the supply lines of the British to Upper Canada. |
| August 30 | Massacre at Fort Mims ignites the Creek War in the South/Southwest. |
| August 31 | Governor Isaac Shelby leaves Newport, Kentucky, with four thousand Kentucky militia plus wives and slaves in retaliation for the River Raisin massacre. A pig goes with them. |
| September 10 | Admiral Oliver Hazard Perry defeats British forces for control in the Battle of Lake Erie. |
| October 5 | The Battle of the Thames routs the British and Native Americans. Tecumseh is killed. Plans for negotiations to end the War of 1812 begin. |
| October 26 | American general Wade Hampton loses the Battle of Châteauguay to Mohawk and Canadian forces as part of the plan to capture Montreal. |
| November 11 | General James Wilkinson loses the Battle of Chrysler's Farm to Canadians and Mohawks as part of the plan to capture Montreal. |
| December 19 | British troops capture Fort Niagara when American brigadier general George McClure withdraws across the Niagara River, ending the campaign to capture Canada for the Americans. |

# 1814

| | |
|---|---|
| April 4 | Napoleon abdicates and is exiled to Elba off the coast of Tuscany, leaving Great Britain free to turn its focus on the war in America. |
| July 3 | American troops cross the Niagara River and capture Fort Erie. |
| July 5 | During the Battle of Chippawa, Americans force the British to withdraw into Canada. |

| July 22 | The Treaty of Greenville is signed, forging peace and friendship between the United States of America and the tribes of Native Americans called the Wyandots, Delawares, Shawanoese, Senacas and Miamies. |
| July 25 | The Battle of Lundy's Lane is one of the fiercest battles of the war, bloody and inconclusive, forcing the Americans to withdraw from Canada. |
| August 8 | Negotiations begin in Ghent, Belgium, to end the War of 1812. |
| August 24 | British troops burn Washington, D.C., including the Capitol. |
| September 13–14 | During the bombardment of Fort McHenry, Francis Scott Key writes the first lines of the poem that becomes "The Star-Spangled Banner." |
| December 1 | Peace negotiators reconvene at Ghent. |
| December 14 | The Hartford Convention is called, a secret meeting of Federalist delegates from Connecticut, Rhode Island, Massachusetts, New Hampshire and Vermont who are dissatisfied with President Madison's mercantile policies and the progress of the war. |
| December 24 | The Treaty of Ghent is signed. |
| December 28 | Great Britain ratifies the Treaty of Ghent. |

# 1815

| January 5 | The Hartford Convention concludes, due to the Treaty of Ghent. |
| January 8 | American and British forces engage in the Battle of New Orleans, unaware the war is over. |
| February 16 | The United States ratifies the Treaty of Ghent. |

| February 18 | The Treaty of Ghent is declared, ending the War of 1812. |
| February 10 | USS *Constitution* engages HMS *Cyane* and HMS *Levant*, not knowing the war is over. |

Chapter 2

# A NEW NATION

In 1812, the United States of America was only thirty-six years old, although it took the European colonists nearly three hundred years to establish a new nation. "In 1492, Columbus sailed the ocean blue," or so the story goes. But Columbus and his Spanish fleet did not sail to what is today the United States. It would take a few more years before Europeans settled in what would become the United States, and nearly every European country wanted in on the New World's potential.

## COLONIALISM

More riches, more land, more resources were the goals of the relentless march for colonial expansion. And that expansion didn't take long to press outward over mountains, down rivers and through forests, adding territory to existing colonies as European immigrants moved westward. Kentucky and West Virginia were part of Virginia, providing furs, land, lumber, wildlife and more to the fledgling colonies. Kentucky has, then, been an integral part of America's history from the very beginning.

British companies funded disenchanted and adventurous Englishmen to make money to fill corporate coffers. Groups suffering religious persecution, those convicted of crimes and enterprising young men and women rushed to the new land in droves to reinvent themselves. During the eighteenth

This Courier & Ives lithograph is titled *A Friendly Campfire*. Fanny F. Palmer, artist. 1860–70. *Courtesy of LOC 92516020.*

century, Britain was entrenched in a contest pitting France and England against each other, and the lucrative colonies were helping fund the fight with taxes, levies and shipments of goods.

## THE BLOODY SEVENS

As migrating Europeans pushed across the Alleghenies, the flames of rebellion spread west into Kentucky. British activities in the war fell on the shoulders of Lieutenant Colonel Henry Hamilton, who was charged with maintaining control of the Ohio River Valley and Canada for England. With few troops at his disposal, Hamilton depended heavily on alliances with Native tribes that inhabited the area for military support. By putting pressure on the Americans with Indian attacks in what is now Kentucky, Hamilton hoped to divert troops from the colonies and thus weaken the Continental army.

In 1777, known as the Year of the Bloody Sevens, Shawnee war chief Blackfish led a force of two hundred warriors across the Ohio River into Western Virginia. Beginning in April and continuing throughout July,

*Daniel Boone Escorting Settlers through the Cumberland Gap* by George Caleb Bingham. 1851. *Courtesy of Wikimedia.*

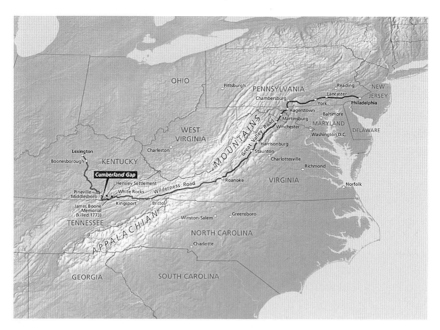

Map showing the Wilderness Trail through the Cumberland Gap. Samuel Valentin Hunt, engraver; Harry Fenn, artist. 1872. *Courtesy of NPS.org.*

This wood engraving demonstrates the danger for immigrants crossing the Appalachian Mountains. 1884. *Courtesy of LOC 2006683701.*

Blackfish struck at Harrodsburg, Boonesborough and St. Asaph's, among others. Rather than launch full-scale assaults on people, the warriors destroyed crops, animals and foodstuffs to compel the Americans to abandon Kentucky. Harassment of forts allowed Native raiding parties to withdraw back across the Ohio River quickly. George Rogers Clark described those dark days at Harrodsburg in his memoir:

> *No people could be in a more alarming situation. Detached at least two hundred miles from the nearest settlements of the states, surrounded by numerous nations of Indians, each one far superior to ourselves in numbers and under the influence of the British government and pointedly directed to destroy us.*

Virginia governor Patrick Henry kept a close eye on the operations in Kentucky, annexed as a county of Virginia in 1776. Henry authorized Colonel George Rogers Clark to launch a strike against the Native Americans allied with the British. Clark assembled a force at the Falls of the Ohio in the spring of 1777 to attack warrior towns in Illinois and relieve the pressure on Kentucky settlements. Clark set out on his expedition at the end of June, capturing Cahokia and Kaskaskia. After a grueling 240-mile march,

Clark and his men surrounded British general Hamilton, who had planned to launch his campaign that spring. Unable to endure a siege, Hamilton surrendered three days later.

While Clark operated in Illinois, Boone was captured at Salt Lick by the Shawnee in June 1778 and managed to escape and return to Boonesborough. Blackfish and a small army appeared in the second week of September to negotiate an end to the fighting. When truce talks broke down, the Shawnees initiated a siege. After twelve days of action, Blackfish abandoned the effort. The Siege of Boonesborough became the most prolonged sustained fight of the American Revolution in what was to become Kentucky.

Despite Clark's victories in Illinois, raids continued throughout the summer of 1780. Finally, the surrender of Lord Cornwallis to General George Washington at Yorktown in October 1781 brought an uneasy calm to Kentucky. But not for long.

Because the opening of Kentucky to settlement happened about the same time the American Revolution began, Kentucky became a battlefield for two different groups.

The British, who also opposed the movement of settlers into Kentucky, gave the Indians weapons and other supplies plus leadership. Sometimes British and Canadian soldiers joined the Indians on raids into Kentucky. Kentuckians responded by fortifying their settlements and organizing militia companies that could be called into action quickly. Every age-appropriate Kentucky male was pressed into service. That first generation of Kentuckians built a reputation as natural fighters. Men like Daniel Boone, James Harrod and Simon Kenton gained international fame as officers in the Kentucky Militia. Known as Kaintucks, these leather-and-linen fighting men became the stereotype of those living in Kentucky.

George Rogers Clark provided the Kentucky Militia with leadership and strategic vision, deciding to take the fight to the Indians. His patrols along the Ohio River, with men on horseback and in boats, helped protect Kentucky settlements from British and Indian attacks from outside.

But nothing could protect Kentucky completely, as the last bloody episode of the Revolution in Kentucky showed. In 1782, a force of about 360 Indians and Canadians loyal to Britain slipped into Kentucky. They attacked the fort at Bryan's Station, near Lexington. Unable to capture the fort, they headed back north.

A pursuing force of Kentuckians walked into an ambush at Blue Licks. In this battle, about sixty-six Kentucky militiamen were killed, including Israel Boone, son of Daniel Boone. Daniel Boone's letter to Virginia's Governor

An illustration of Daniel Boone at the Battle of Blue Licks in *Indian History for Young Folks* by Francis Samuel Drake. 1919. *Courtesy of Wikimedia.*

Benjamin Harrison V described the last battle of the Revolution fought in Kentucky and asked for assistance as Kentucky continued to battle the British and Indians.

> *Boone's Station, Fayette Co. August 30th, 1782.*
> *SIR,—Present circumstances of affairs cause me to write to your Excellency as follows. On the 16th instant a large number of Indians with some white men attacked one of our frontier stations known by the name of Bryant's [sic] Station. The siege continued from about sunrise till about ten o'clock the next day....By the sign we thought the Indians had exceeded four hundred; while the whole of this militia of the county does not amount*

*to more than one hundred and thirty. From these facts your Excellency may form an idea of our situation. I know that your own circumstances are critical, but are we to be wholly forgotten? I hope not. I trust about five hundred men may be sent to our assistance immediately. If these shall be stationed as our county lieutenants shall deem necessary, it may be the means of saving our part of the country; but if they are placed under the direction of Gen. Clark, they will be of little or no service to our settlement. The Falls lie one hundred miles west of us and the Indians northeast; while our men are frequently called to protect them. I have encouraged the people in this country all that I could, but I can no longer justify them or myself to risk our lives here under such extraordinary hazards. The inhabitants of this county are very much alarmed at the thoughts of the Indians bringing another campaign into our country this Fall. If this should be the case, it will break up these settlements. I hope therefore your Excellency will take the matter into your consideration, and send us some relief as quick as possible. These are my sentiments without consulting any person. Col. Logan will I expect, immediately send you an express, by whom I humbly request your Excellency's answer—in the mean while I remain, Daniel Boone*

The August 19, 1782 battle was the last victory for the Loyalists and Natives during the frontier portion of the Revolutionary War.

## THE SECOND GREAT AWAKENING

By the late 1700s, thirteen British colonies, including the part of Virginia that would become Kentucky, were growing increasingly dissatisfied with how England governed them. The same dissatisfaction that led the immigrants to America was being inflamed by religious fervor during what is known as the Second Great Awakening, a religious reform movement led by Protestant ministers that began in Kentucky. To immigrants in the early nineteenth century, the land in the United States seemed pristine; in *Discovering Our Roots: The Ancestry of the Churches of Christ*, it is referred to as "the perfect place to recover pure, uncorrupted and original Christianity." The tradition-bound, authoritarian European churches were out of place in this new setting. Moreover, the large numbers of Scots-Irish funneled into Eastern Kentucky with land grants were generally characterized as reflecting acute individualism, dislike of aristocracy, a strong military tradition and religious piety. And so it was that Kentucky was the epicenter of this Second Great Awakening.

This drawing typifies a rural camp meeting held in Kentucky in the early 1800s. Drawn on stone. Circa 1829. *Courtesy of LOC 96510018.*

Cane Ridge was the site, in 1801, of a huge camp meeting that drew thousands of people and had a lasting influence. Located in what is now Bourbon County near Paris, Kentucky, the ridge was named by the explorer Daniel Boone, who noticed a form of bamboo growing there.

An estimated twenty thousand people attended throughout the week, and Presbyterian, Baptist and Methodist ministers preached across the campsite, often standing on stumps as pulpits. Based on Scottish traditions of Holy Fairs, the meeting began with preaching on Friday evening through Saturday, with communion starting on Sunday. Over one thousand individuals are estimated to have taken communion at this camp meeting.

Individualism and social justice issues were growing, building support systems that focused on American institutions and salvation, apart from European dominance. Horace Walpole, an English man of letters during the Revolutionary period, summed up the change in temperament in the colonies. As quoted in the *Journal of the Presbyterian Historical Society*, Walpole told Parliament, "There is no use crying about it. Cousin America has run off with a Presbyterian parson, and that is the end of it."

# One War Ends

The Treaty of Paris ended the Revolutionary War in 1783, establishing the United States of America as the first nation-state characterized by elections between multiple distinct political parties, a separation of powers into different branches of government, the rule of law in everyday life and the equal protection of human rights, civil rights, civil liberties and political freedoms for all people.

A new nation was born with thirteen states:

Connecticut
Delaware
Georgia
Maryland
Massachusetts
New Hampshire
New Jersey
New York
North Carolina
Pennsylvania
Rhode Island
South Carolina
Virginia (which included the area of Kentucky)

And the nation immediately began to grow. By 1812, there were five additional states:

1791: Vermont
1792: Kentucky
1796: Tennessee
1803: Ohio
1812: Louisiana

# Continued Trouble

But the troubles were far from over. For three decades after the United States separated from Britain, enmity between France, Spain, the Dutch Republic and England created a massive headache for America. Neither France,

England nor Spain recognized the United States as its own nation and saw it as taking sides with one or the other.

If American ships were found in European ports, they were considered enemy vessels (allied with France) by the Royal Navy and were fired on. Similarly, if American ships were trading in British ports, France considered them the enemy and attacked. Goods were stolen, sailors and passengers were killed and general havoc ensued. Both Britain and France wanted exclusive trading rights, and Britain and France each wanted to weaken the other through the denial of trade with the new United States of America.

Well into the new century, the Royal Navy's use of impressment to keep its ships fully crewed provoked Americans. The British raided American merchant ships looking for Royal Navy deserters, carrying off thousands of U.S. citizens in the process. Between 1803 and 1812, historian Brian Walter Bornean estimates the British navy captured between five and nine thousand American sailors at sea and "pressed" them into service.

By the early nineteenth century, the British were also amassing a front in the Northwest Territories to regain or at least prevent further expansion into their lands. Native tribes, with charismatic new leaders for their Pan-Indian Confederacy Tecumseh and his brother Tenskwatawa, were beginning to band together to stop the onslaught of White settlers and their push into tribal lands.

Kentucky was keenly aware of the impact of the British-Indian Alliance and Pan-Indian Confederacy on immigrant settlers flooding the region beside them. The Year of the Bloody Sevens had shown them intimately the trials those settlers faced. They'd been through it themselves, all too recently.

The *Kentucky Encyclopedia* describes Kentucky's response to the outbreak of the War of 1812 as "enthusiastic." Kentucky's political representatives were for the war; many even volunteered to serve in the field. By September 1812, Governor Isaac Shelby was turning away militia volunteers for lack of weapons and equipment.

The United States was feeling isolated, harassed, besieged and pressured. The world still saw it as a colony to be manipulated and beleaguered. Yet with the U.S. population in 1812 more than seven million people, Americans could boast they now lived in the largest country in the civilized world after Russia and the only independent republic. And by 1812, the Founding Fathers were fed up and making their feelings known.

Saying you were an independent, sovereign nation was one thing. Defending it was quite another.

Chapter 3

# KENTUCKY BEFORE 1812

From the initial rumblings in Washington in support of a "Second War of Independence" by Kentuckian Henry Clay, leading the War Hawks, through the massacres of Kentucky militias at Fort Meigs and River Raisin to the Battle of the Thames, which jumpstarted the negotiations toward the Treaty of Ghent that ended the war, to the Battle of New Orleans, Kentuckians featured prominently. In so many ways, the War of 1812 was Kentucky's War.

## NATIVE OCCUPANCY

The land now called Kentucky was occupied by humans far before European settlement. Modern archaeologists classify Kentucky's prehistoric past into six cultures: the Paleo-Indian culture, the Archaic culture, the Woodland culture, the Adena culture, the Mississippian culture and the Fort Ancient culture. Until the arrival of the first White settlers, Indigenous wars were frequently fought over control of the "Great Meadow" between the Shawnee tribes from north of the Ohio River and the Cherokee and Chickasaw tribes located south of the Cumberland River. While the area was commonly visited as a hunting ground, modern investigators believe that no Indian nation actually held possession of the land that eventually became Kentucky.

By 1650, the rivers of the Mississippi basin, primarily the Ohio River, were frequently traveled by fur traders and hunters. Native resistance and rough,

Mississippian culture pottery from the Wickliffe Mounds site in western Kentucky. *Permission of Herb Roe, www.chromesun.com.*

*Rest of the Traveler.* Alphonse Legros, artist. *Public domain. Owned by Cleveland Museum of Art. Made available under the Creative Commons CC0 1.0. Courtesy of Wikimedia.*

heavily wooded terrain hindered exploration. The Proclamation of 1763 by Great Britain forbade settlement beyond the Appalachian Mountains and required those who had made their home there to leave.

In 1768, lands west of the Alleghenies and south of the Ohio River were ceded to the colonies by the Cherokee at the Treaty of Hard Labour and by the Six Nations at the Treaty of Fort Stanwix. However, some Indigenous nations, particularly the Shawnee and Mingo, stayed put and claimed their lands had been sold without permission by other tribes.

These and other treaties and agreements ignored the preexisting claims of the Cherokee, Shawnee and Iroquois. When the Treaty of Sycamore Shoals with the Natives was signed in 1775, Cherokee chief Dragging Canoe refused to endorse the sale. Legendary historian Lewis Collins and many others tell that he warned the Transylvania Company they were purchasing a "dark and bloody ground."

## THE LAND GRAB

The first colonial explorers into the Appalachian Plateau left little indication of their presence and caused few upsets among the Indigenous inhabitants. The first documentation of a crossing through the Cumberland Gap is the 1750 journal of Dr. Thomas Walker, a key member of the Loyal Land Company and the person who, with fellow surveyor Christopher Gist, established the state's southern boundary—the Walker Line—as an extension of the Virginia-North Carolina boundary.

Walker was exploring the mountains to determine what areas to advertise, survey and sell. The Loyal Land Company Syndicate provided a grant that came at no cost but required lands to be surveyed within four years. The syndicate would gain revenue only if settlers purchased individual parcels. Walker also identified possible routes that would be used to cross the mountains, which is why he examined and named Cumberland Gap.

Daniel Boone visited Kentucky on a 1767 expedition. He was so impressed that he vowed to return. And in 1769, with a party of hunters led by John Finley, he returned for a two-year exploration and survey of the region. In 1774, James Harrod constructed the first permanent settlement in Kentucky at Fort Harrod, the site of present-day Harrodsburg. Boonesborough was established in 1775, and many other settlements were created soon after. From its very beginnings, Kentucky was a place for the adventurous and courageous, unafraid and undeterred by the prospects of a hardscrabble life.

Engraving of Cumberland Gap. S.V. Hunt, engraver; Harry Fenn, artist; circa 1872. *Courtesy of LOC 95513932.*

Bardstown, Kentucky, has created a frontier village near the military museum. *Courtesy of Dixie Hibbs.*

During those early days, every able-bodied man was considered a member of the militia as a part-time soldier. They were farmers, merchants or tradesmen who took up arms to protect their homes and families—and the homes and families of others—during emergencies. And there were plenty of emergencies. The Indians saw the Kentucky settlements as the beginning of an invasion of their priceless hunting grounds. When Daniel Boone moved his family, including his wife and children, to Boonesborough—in present-day Madison County—it marked a new era in the frontier—a shift to families laying permanent claim to the land. Kentuckians and the Indians fought each other, off and on, for more than forty years. As Chief Dragging Canoe had predicted, Kentucky indeed became a "dark and bloody ground."

In 1786, Simon Kenton created the Kentucky Minutemen, who covered northern Kentucky from April until November, the months most subject to Indian attack. During this period, the militiamen became known as the "Limestone Volunteers." The Kentucky Board of War was created in 1791, enlisting men in service for active duty for a three-month term. William Whitley, killed in action during the Battle of the Thames twenty years later,

Bill Smith, an 1812 reenactor, takes aim with a Peter Gunter Jr. (1751–1818) long rifle made in Lancaster around 1808. *Author's collection.*

The Kentucky long rifle was accurate but gave the militiaman a face full of black smoke with each shot. Dana Stiefel. *Public domain. Courtesy of River Raisin National Battlefield Park, NPS.gov.*

joined with the Tennessee Territorial Militia to defeat the Chickamauga Indians, greatly diminishing the scope and threat of attack in Western and Southern Kentucky.

Known as the Cornstalk Militia, these raw recruits bore with them a truly unique rifle, the Kentucky long rifle—a muzzle-loading firearm characterized by a very long barrel of relatively small caliber but using rifling (spiral grooves in the bore) to cause the round lead ball to spin around the axis of its motion. This technique dramatically improved the long rifle's stability of trajectory and accuracy over those of smoothbore muskets, which were cheaper and more common. Any self-respecting Kentuckian carried one.

## THE NATIVE RESPONSE

The Indians responded by sending fast-moving raiding parties into Kentucky from their villages north of the Ohio River. They burned homes and crops, slaughtered livestock and killed or kidnapped settlers. Between 1675 and 1763, over 1,600 Whites in New England were abducted by Native Americans.

More often than not, it was women and children who bore the brunt of these captures, frequently initiated to replace tribal members lost to fighting with Whites. Generally, these captives were meant to be assimilated into the tribe, so—although closely watched—they were treated well.

But the culture change meant it could be a brutal life for a female captive, and many died as a result. Some had better luck than others and were traded or ransomed back to their families. Others staged daring escapes, preferring

31

to face the elements rather than live among their captors. And some simply accepted their lot, making the tribal lifestyle their own.

On July 14, 1776, two weeks after the signing of the Declaration of Independence, Jemima Boone and two friends were occupied like many girls their age—escaping chores and testing parental boundaries. The three girls came upon the settlement's only canoe and decided to take a ride across the river. When the girls drifted too close to the opposite shore, a Cherokee-Shawnee raiding party captured the girls. Hanging Maw, the raiders' leader, recognized Jemima Boone and realized she could be a valuable pawn in the battle to drive her father's settlement out of the territory for good. But his plans were thwarted when her father and eight men ambushed the raiding party and rescued the girls.

President Abraham Lincoln's grandfather, for whom he is named, was killed in the early moments of a raid on his four-hundred-acre tract near Hughes Station in eastern Jefferson County. In May 1786, Abraham was planting corn with his sons, Josiah, Mordecai and Thomas (Honest Abe's father), when they were attacked by a small war party. Mordecai ran into

Daniel Boone and his friends rescuing his daughter Jemima from Hanging Maw. 1851. Associated name on shelflist card: Nagel & Weingartner. *Courtesy of LOC 2003656944.*

the cabin to get a rifle, returning just in time to kill the Indian preparing to scalp his dead father.

Jenny Wiley's name graces a number of books, an outdoor drama and a state park, and she has lent her name to businesses throughout Eastern Kentucky. Seven months pregnant, Jenny was seized by Natives when her husband was away on or around the first of October 1789. A letter dated October 20 from Montgomery County lieutenant Walter Crockett to Virginia governor Beverley Randolph reads: "On the first of this instant A party of Indians took one Willey's [sic] family, killed and scalped foure [sic] of his children and took his wife and her youngest child prisoners."

Jenny was forced to watch her remaining two children, one born during captivity, killed in front of her. Her capture and subsequent escape became a watchword for families in the area during that period. Mothers calling "Jenny Wiley" out to their children meant for them to come home immediately because danger was afoot.

These events are far from unique. America's unsettled lands called to those searching for fortune, adventure or a fresh start. But immigrants faced atrocities committed by both Natives and Europeans. According to historians of the era, settlers seized by Natives during America's four centuries of westward expansion number in the tens of thousands.

Neither the end of the Revolution nor the achievement of Kentucky statehood—it separated from Virginia in 1792—brought peace to Kentucky. The British remained in place near the Canadian border and continued to support the Indians in their opposition to American growth between the Appalachians and the Mississippi River, focusing now on the Northwest Territory (Ohio, Indiana, Illinois, Michigan, Wisconsin). The new United States government sent several expeditions, which included many Kentucky militiamen, against the Indians, which only inflamed their opponents in the ensuing two decades.

## THE SCOTS-IRISH FLOOD

Meanwhile, Kentucky was being inundated with new residents-to-be. From 1780 to 1790 alone, historians estimate more than one hundred thousand immigrants passed through the Cumberland Gap. Part of the reason was that the brand-new United States of America did not have the funds to pay Patriots for their service, so a system of land warrants was devised as remuneration, and free land was a huge draw. The Kentucky secretary of state's website provides a database that indicates 4,748 bounty land warrants were issued by Virginia between August 8, 1782, and October 29, 1793, to veterans of the Revolutionary War. Warrants, the first step in land patenting, were given as payment for military services; the allotment was determined by the soldier's rank and time of service, and the land was located in the Revolutionary War Military District:

> *bounded by the Green River and a southeast course from the head thereof to the Cumberland mountains, with the said mountains to the Carolina line, with the Carolina line to the Cherokee or Tennessee River, with the said river to the Ohio River, and with the Ohio to the said Green River, until the farther order of the general assembly.*

Each state determined its veterans' land allotment. Legislation by the Virginia General Assembly and research by Lloyd DeWitt Bockstruck indicates Virginia paid the following bounties for service in the Revolutionary War:

| | |
|---|---|
| Sailor or soldier who served three-year enlistment | 100 acres |
| Noncommissioned officer who served three-year enlistment | 200 acres |
| Sailor or soldier who served throughout the war | 400 acres |
| Noncommissioned officer who served throughout the war | 400 acres |
| Subaltern-Cornet | 2,000 to 2,666 acres |
| Subaltern-Ensign | 2,000 to 2,666 acres |
| Subaltern-Lieutenant | 2,000 to 2,666 acres |
| Surgeon's Mate | 2,666 to 8,000 acres |
| Surgeon | 2,666 to 8,000 acres |
| Chaplain | 2,666 to 8,000 acres |
| Captain | 3,000 to 4,666 acres |
| Major | 4,000 to 5,333 acres |

| Lieutenant Colonel | 4,500 to 6,666 acres |
| --- | --- |
| Colonel | 5,000 to 8,888 acres |
| Brigadier General | 10,000 acres+ |
| Major General | 15,000 to 17,500 acres |

When any officer, soldier or sailor fell or died in the service, his heirs or legal representatives were entitled to and received the same quantity of land as would have been due the officer, soldier or sailor had he been living. Other state warrant registries provided similar grants for their soldiers given land grants in Kentucky.

In 1773, the royal governor of Virginia, Lord Dunmore, overruled objections from Fincastle County officials. He approved private surveys for land claims at the highly desirable area of the Falls of the Ohio River (now Louisville). He also declared that military warrants, which entitled officers and soldiers who fought in the French and Indian War to land grants, could be filed anywhere in Virginia.

Many Kentucky families can trace their ancestry back to land grants given to these soldiers of primarily British Isles descent, which bears out today through DNA. More than a half-million Eastern Kentuckians who took Ancestry's DNA test share a similar genetic heritage. As recently as 1980, more than 80 percent of Eastern Kentuckians surveyed attributed their ancestry primarily to the British Isles.

Eastern Kentucky, in particular, has strong Scots-Irish heritage. Hardy and independent, with a fighting spirit and family-centric philosophy, Scots-Irish settlers kept going beyond settled areas to find greater religious freedom, tolerance and independence and the opportunity to build their own communities. While the Scots-Irish were not openly hostile to other cultures, they separated themselves by culture and religion and thus tended not to intermarry or socialize with other groups.

These early Americans took several routes to end up in Appalachia. The Scots-Irish followed the Great Wagon Road that traversed the six hundred miles from Pennsylvania to Georgia, many settling along that path.

The Shenandoah Valley of Virginia became a launching point for further migration to the Carolinas, Georgia, Tennessee and Kentucky, primarily of Scots-Irish. Eventually, with so many Scots-Irish settling in Appalachia, Charleston became the second-most important arrival port (after New York) for ships from Ireland.

Closely related peoples from the borderlands of England, Scotland, Ireland and Wales—called Borderers—encompassed a number of other settlers who shared many of the same traits and were welcomed into the new homeland by the previous settlers.

## A VIRGINIA APPENDAGE

Virginia's claim to the land comes from the Second Charter issued to the Virginia Company signed by King James III in 1609. That charter theoretically set the western edge of the territory at the Pacific Ocean. However, the 1763 Treaty of Paris ending the Seven Years' or French and Indian War set the boundary at the Mississippi River as the western edge because the Crown accepted Spain's claim to lands on the west side of—and including—the Mississippi River.

On New Year's Eve, 1776, the area of Virginia beyond the Appalachian Mountains known as Fincastle County was designated as Kentucky County, alternately spelled Kentucke County. The precise etymology of the name is uncertain but is likely based on an Iroquoian word meaning "on the meadow" or "on the prairie," from the Mohawk Kenhta-ke, or Seneca gëdá'geh, "at the field," from the Mohawk kĕtaʔkeh.

Others have put forth "Kentaki" as a possible source, which derives from the Algonquian language and, therefore, was derived from the Shawnee. Folk etymology states that this translates to "Land of Our Fathers." The closest approximation is in another Algonquian language, Ojibwe (in northern Michigan), which translates it to "Land of Our In-Laws," thus making a fairer English translation "Land of Those Who Became Our Fathers."

During the three and a half years Kentucky County was part of the Commonwealth of Virginia, its seat of government was Harrodstown (then also known as Oldtown, later renamed Harrodsburg). On June 30, 1780, the Virginia House of Delegates renamed Kentucky County, Virginia, as the District of Kentucky and divided it into:

FAYETTE COUNTY: Named for the Marquis de Lafayette (1757–1834)—who came to America at the age of nineteen to support the rebelling English colonies in the American Revolutionary War. His actions as a nobleman of an established and respected European nation gave great strength to the Patriots.

JEFFERSON COUNTY: Named for President Thomas Jefferson (1743–1826)—who was governor of Virginia at the time of its creation. Respect and desire to honor Jefferson were widespread during the county division.

LINCOLN COUNTY: Named for Revolutionary War general Benjamin Lincoln (1733–1810)—who served as a major general in the Continental army and who formally accepted the British surrender at Yorktown. He was not related to President Abraham Lincoln.

As the war for independence approached, Lord Dunsmore resigned, and rebel leaders took over management of the Commonwealth. Like their British counterparts, they were reluctant to reduce their stores of arms and munitions by sending them to frontier settlers west of the Cumberland Gap. It took George Rogers Clark going in person to Williamsburg to request supplies. The Virginia leaders still said no. Ever the wily Kentuckian, Clark suggested to Governor Patrick Henry that Kentucky residents might have to negotiate a deal with the Spanish or French (who still had their eyes on the territory) for aid if Virginia was unwilling to provide it. In his missive to Henry, Clark wrote, "I was sorry to find we should have to seek protection elsewhere, which I do not doubt of getting, that if a country was not worth protecting it was not worth claiming."

Very quickly, Virginia made sure that guns and ammunition were on the way through the Cumberland Gap to the beleaguered settlers.

## QUEST FOR STATEHOOD

Almost from the beginning, Kentucky petitioned both the Virginia legislature and the Continental Congress seeking statehood. Constitution Square in Danville was the site of the ten constitutional conventions that led to Kentucky's statehood. The frontier politicians who lived in what was then the Kentucky County of Virginia struggled for more than eight years for independence, gathering in Constitution Square in Danville to draft, then submit draft after draft of their application for statehood.

Several factors contributed to the desire of Kentuckians to separate from Virginia. First, the journey to the Virginia state capital from Kentucky was long and dangerous. Using local militias against Indian raids required authorization and munitions from the governor of Virginia. But perhaps most importantly, Virginia refused to recognize the importance of Mississippi River trade to Kentucky's economy. It forbade trade with the Spanish colony of New Orleans (which controlled the mouth of the Mississippi) but was critical to get Kentucky goods to buyers. Until the steamship was invented (by Kentuckian John Fitch) and navigating both directions on waterways was possible decades later, the fastest and most economical way to transport products was by flatboat down the Mississippi to New Orleans and then on

A statue of Isaac Shelby and a frontiersman generally regarded as Daniel Boone overlooks Constitution Square in downtown Danville, Kentucky. *Author's collection.*

to the goods' destination. Traversing the Cumberland Gap had too many barriers to even consider.

Problems increased with rapid population growth in Kentucky, leading Colonel Benjamin Logan to call the first constitutional convention in Danville in 1784. Over the next several years, nine more constitutional conventions were held. During one, General James Wilkinson unsuccessfully proposed secession from Virginia and the United States for Kentucky to become a Spanish possession, a plot known as the Spanish Conspiracy.

In 1788, Virginia consented to Kentucky statehood with two enabling acts, the second of which required the Confederation Congress to admit Kentucky into the United States by July 4, 1788. A committee of the whole recommended that Kentucky be admitted, and the United States Congress took up the question of Kentucky statehood on July 3. But on July 2, Congress learned about New Hampshire's ratification of the proposed constitution, and so it resolved

> *that the said Legislature and the inhabitants of the district aforesaid* [Kentucky] *be informed, that as the constitution of the United States is now ratified, Congress think it unadviseable* [sic] *to adopt any further measures for admitting the district of Kentucky into the federal Union as an independent member thereof under the Articles of Confederation and perpetual Union; but that Congress thinking it expedient that the said district be made a separate State and member of the Union as soon after proceedings shall commence under the said constitution as circumstances shall permit, recommend it to the said legislature and to the inhabitants of the said district so to alter their acts and resolutions relative to the premises* [sic] *as to render them conformable to the provisions made in the said constitution to the End that no impediment may be in the way of the speedy accomplishment of this important business.*

Kentucky's final push for statehood (now under the new U.S. Constitution) began with an April 1792 convention, again in Danville. Delegates drafted the tenth and final Kentucky Constitution and submitted it to Congress.

The document that the convention drafted included several relatively new and progressive features. Two such features were the provisions that called for conducting all elections by ballot rather than by the widely used voice vote of the times and basing representation of both houses of the general assembly on population rather than geography.

Finally, on June 1, 1792, Kentucky became the fifteenth state in the Union, and Isaac Shelby, a Revolutionary War hero and convention delegate, was named the first governor of the new commonwealth. A statue of Shelby and what is widely considered Daniel Boone stands in a raised garden bed with plaques of Shelby's virtues, overlooking colonial-style buildings reconstructing Constitution Square in Danville. This image appears on the Kentucky state seal with the motto "United we stand, divided we fall." Shelby's fondness for John Dickinson's "The Liberty Song" is believed to be the reason Kentucky adopted the state motto.

## THE NEW MADRID SHAKEUP

Kentucky was about to experience a shakeup of a completely different sort, one that would be physically felt across the central and eastern United States. At the point where Missouri, Tennessee, Arkansas, Illinois and Kentucky come together, the 1811–1812 New Madrid (mædrɪd/) earthquakes, named for the river town of New Madrid, began with an initial earthquake of between 7.2 and 8.2 on December 16, 1811, followed by a 7.4 aftershock on the same day. Two additional earthquakes of similar magnitude followed in January and February 1812. They remain the most powerful earthquakes to hit the contiguous United States east of the Rocky Mountains in recorded history.

Eyewitnesses declared they saw the Mississippi River flow backward during the quakes, likely an optical illusion due to heavy waves and rising/falling water levels. As recorded by historian Lewis Collins, Eliza Bryan, who resided in New Madrid, wrote the following eyewitness account in March 1812:

> On the 16th of December, 1811, about two o'clock, a.m., we were visited by a violent shock of an earthquake, accompanied by a very awful noise resembling loud but distant thunder, but more hoarse and vibrating, which was followed in a few minutes by the complete saturation of the atmosphere, with sulphurious vapor, causing total darkness. The screams of the affrighted inhabitants running to and fro, not knowing where to go, or what to do—the cries of the fowls and beasts of every species—the cracking of trees falling, and the roaring of the Mississippi— the current of which was retrograde for a few minutes, owing as is supposed, to an irruption in its bed—formed a scene truly horrible.

Fortunately, the epicenters of the earthquakes were only sparsely settled. Compared to a similar event occurring today, the loss of life and buildings was slight. Seismologists estimate that today such an event could kill or maim more than eighty-six thousand people and would generate a loss of upward of $300 billion in most of the eastern United States.

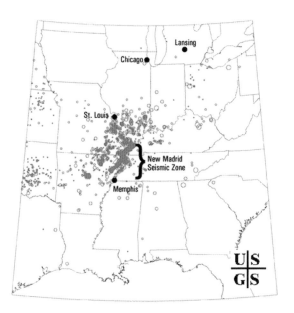

*Top*: The 1811–12 New Madrid earthquakes in the New Madrid Seismic Zone, centered in New Madrid County, Missouri. *United States Geological Survey. Courtesy of Wikimedia.*

*Middle*: Drawing of a cabin being destroyed by the New Madrid earthquakes. Creator unknown; published 1851 in a book by Henry Howe. *Courtesy of Wikimedia.*

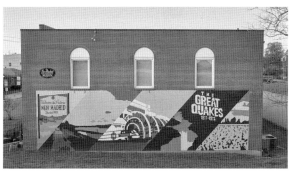

*Bottom*: A mural in New Madrid (pronounced *Mad*-rid) documents when it was the epicenter of powerful earthquakes and aftershocks in 1811 and 1812. *Courtesy of LOC 2020742444.*

A map of the Kentucky Bend exclave between Missouri and Tennessee, USA. Jim Efaw, creator. *Made available by Creative Commons Attribution-Share Alike 2.5. Courtesy of Wikimedia.*

Interestingly, Kentucky has a noncontiguous piece of land known as Kentucky Bend, or Bubbleland, at the far western corner of the state, which most people believe results from the earthquakes. It's an exclave surrounded by Missouri and Tennessee and included in the boundaries of Fulton County, Kentucky. Road access to this small part of Kentucky on the Mississippi River (populated by eighteen people as of 2010) requires a trip through Tennessee. The epicenter of the powerful 1811–12 New Madrid earthquakes was near this area. While the series of quakes did change the area geologically, the Kentucky Bend was formed because of a surveying error, not the New Madrid earthquake as is generally thought.

Geologists today frequently wonder about the likelihood of a recurrence in our lifetimes. Experts currently estimate the possibility of another earthquake the magnitude of the 1811–12 New Madrid earthquakes in the next fifty years as 70–80 percent for one of 7+ magnitude and 25–40 percent for one of 6+ magnitude.

Coming on the heels of Tecumseh's push for Natives to band together against the Whites, the New Madrid earthquakes were interpreted in various ways by American Indian tribes. Still, one consensus was universally accepted: the powerful earthquake had to have meant something. For many tribes in Tecumseh's Pan-Indian Confederacy, it meant that Tecumseh and his brother, the Prophet, must be supported. As the European population of Kentucky continued to swell beyond its statehood in 1792 and into the early nineteenth century, Spain, England, Canada and the Native tribes were not happy.

## ABUNDANT RESOURCES

The War of 1812 may not have been fought on Kentucky soil, but the war would have looked very different without the state providing vital resources to the war effort. Kentucky provided most of the human resources for the northwestern front in the war, but more than militia, Kentucky had some significant resources held at two major supply bases. Newport, Kentucky, dubbed Newport Barracks, was the mustering space for troops headed north to fight, and stored much of the needed supplies. Built in 1804 at the juncture of the Licking and Ohio Rivers, the Newport Barracks was an arsenal and recruiting ground. Similarly, Leestown, near Wilkinson Boulevard in Frankfort, Kentucky, was also a supply base for the militia.

The limestone caves of Kentucky became the focal point of a brief—but vital—mining industry in support of the American war effort. Dr. Samuel Brown, a professor at Transylvania University, was doing research on cave niter in the manufacture of gunpowder. According to the historical marker on the Transylvania campus in Lexington, "Dr. Brown's analyses led to the use of Kentucky cave niter in the manufacture of gunpowder. This added to Kentucky's role in winning the War of 1812." Mammoth Cave and the Great Saltpeter Cave were mined extensively to retrieve the organic materials for manufacturing gunpowder after British blockades successfully halted the cheaper imported powders. At Mammoth Cave, whose saltpeter was considered to be of exceptional quality, historians estimate a whopping 570,000 pounds were produced during the war.

The saltpeter manufactured at Mammoth Cave was sold to gunpowder manufacturers to meet American military needs. *Courtesy of the Library of Congress.*

Rich iron ore deposits were discovered in several parts of Kentucky, which brought to the state a measure of industry that was previously lacking. Industrialist entrepreneurs like John Owings took note of the rich resources in the Appalachian Mountains of Eastern Kentucky that would provide the materials for an iron foundry. A decade later, an ironworks furnace was officially established as the Bourbon Iron Works.

The Bourbon Iron Works was an immediate success. Pioneers traversing the Appalachian Mountains had left stoves, furniture, cookware and lamps back East and needed replacements. Iron became even more of a commodity during the War of 1812, when Americans boycotted British goods. So when General Andrew Jackson, anticipating an attack from the British on New Orleans, purchased shipments of cannonballs from the Kentucky furnace, the business became famous. The supplies were loaded on barges and shipped down the Mississippi River. The shipment proved imperative to Jackson's victory at the Battle of New Orleans. Because of this, the Bourbon furnace was dubbed the "Old Thunder Mill" until it was decommissioned in 1838.

Even soldiers need to relax. Olympian Springs, originally known as Mud Lick Springs, was purchased around 1800 by Colonel Thomas Hart, Henry

The Bourbon Iron Works near Owingsville was built in 1791 and today is listed on the National Register of Historic Places. *Courtesy of Wikimedia.*

Clay's father-in-law, who built a hotel, changed the name and promoted the site's health benefits. During the War of 1812, the Twenty-Eighth United States Infantry Regiment camped at the site. Over the next one hundred years, the resort's popularity declined, and by the mid-1940s, it was being used for farmland.

As homes began to dot the Bluegrass, it was natural that the settlers, primarily from Pennsylvania, Virginia and the Carolinas, would bring their love of horse racing (and their prized stock) along with them, as all of them considered horse racing to be a popular sport. Streets and trails were used for horse races, usually straight quarter-mile dash races. These spur-of-the-moment runs could be dangerous for spectators or those walking down the street. According to Kentucky Historic Marker No. 6, Lexington town trustees, writing in 1793:

*Feeling the dangers and inconveniences which are occasioned by the practice, but too common, of racing through the streets led this town meeting to consider the means which ought to be adopted for applying a remedy to this growing evil.*

45

*Left*: A miniature copper still holds the nameplates of the inductees to the Kentucky Bourbon Hall of Fame. *Courtesy of Dixie Hibbs Collection.*

*Below*: Bourbon barrels line the rows of rickhouses throughout the state, lending credence to the idea that there are more barrels of bourbon in Kentucky than people. *Courtesy of Dixie Hibbs Collection.*

And so, racetracks were designed just for horse racing. Before statehood in 1792, Lexington's newspaper, the *Kentucky Gazette*, was reporting on and advertising racing events and offering bloodline horses for sale and stud. Not long after, the move was made to mile-long oval track races, often consisting of multiple heats. These tracks, and their well-attended race days, evolved over the years into such storied Kentucky locations as Churchill Downs and Keeneland.

Of course, no list of Kentucky resources would be complete without referencing America's only native spirit: bourbon. It was likely first distilled near Nelson County, Kentucky, by Baptist preacher Walter (Waddie) Boone, a relative of Daniel living at Pottinger's Creek in Nelson County around 1776. Boone and his partner in Boone's Distillery, Stephen Ritchie, are the likeliest candidates for the inventors of bourbon, although there are a few other contenders. President Abraham Lincoln is said to have delivered lunch to his father, Thomas, when he began working at the distillery in 1814.

By the time the War of 1812 was declared, bourbon was being manufactured throughout Kentucky—legally and illegally—and shipped down the Mississippi to New Orleans for shipment to the East Coast and Europe. Distilled spirits were anesthetic, disinfectant and distraction, and their use in wartime was mandatory.

So at the brink of 1812, Kentuckians were fired up with religious fervor, terrified of the natural world and desirous to master it, fed up with politics, solidifying claim to their territory and expanding a growing economy, and they had gotten enough of a foothold as a state in what was becoming an international power to want to participate in whatever way they could. So when James Madison declared war on Great Britain, Kentucky was ready.

Chapter 4

# ISAAC SHELBY, THE GOVERNOR

Born in Hagerstown, Maryland, to Evan and Letitia Cox Shelby in 1783, Isaac Shelby moved west, settling in Boonesborough and marrying Susannah Hart, with whom he had eleven children. Isaac was brought up with the family traditions of hunting, trapping, fishing, farming and cattle raising, and his father and grandfather before him were active in civic life in the roles of county justice, surveyor, Indian trader and more. The primary aim of the Shelby family, however, was to purchase as much land as they could amass, first in Wales, then in Pennsylvania, Maryland and North Carolina before Isaac settled in what is now Lincoln County, Kentucky, at a farm he called Traveler's Rest. Indeed, for much of his life, this would be his happy place.

Historians relate that Isaac felt he had what he later called "the rudiments of a plain English education." Essentially, in Isaac's world, being literate meant figuring, reading and writing in a basic manner. The schooling of his youth probably lasted no more than a year or two. Isaac and his siblings learned most of what they needed by participating in business around the land and the affairs of their parents. Perhaps this is why he was such a supporter of the first college west of the Alleghenies, Transylvania College—first organized in Danville, then moved to Lexington—and of the later Centre College in Danville.

## SHELBY AS A PATRIOT

The American Revolution, as well as Indian unrest, was brewing around the Virginia/Tennessee/North Carolina site of Isaac Shelby's father's homestead (also named Traveler's Rest), where today stand the twin towns of Bristol, Tennessee, and Bristol, Virginia. The Shelbys and surrounding settlers quickly became embroiled in the skirmishes with the Indians, becoming increasingly aware of the locals' distrust of the British—and chomping at the bit to gain even more territory to the west.

Frequently called the "First Battle of the American Revolution," Lord Dunsmore's War was the Virginia governor's response to Shawnee and Mingo attacks after several Native Americans had been killed. The Shelby family men—including twenty-three-year-old Isaac, recently made a lieutenant—and fifty volunteers from the surrounding settlements began a two-hundred-mile trek north, pausing only to sleep or hunt for meat. On October 9, 1774, Dunsmore's men were attacked, sparking a battle so intense that neither militiamen nor Indians could see through the smoke. In the end, trees were red with blood from both sides, and when Dunsmore came to the bargaining table, the Shawnees and Mingos were ready to agree to his terms. The Indians would keep the lands north of the Ohio River but were not to cross to the south. Not only was this first battle of Isaac's life important to him personally, but it was also critical to his later settlement in the area he came to love.

But first, a war was to be won—one the Patriots were not winning. Isaac Shelby and some one thousand militiamen—without orders, formal military training, uniforms or provisions and with no promise of pay—set out to defeat the supposedly "superior forces" of noted English colonel Patrick Ferguson after receiving a message from his camp in Gilbert Town, North Carolina. In their book on Shelby, Wrobel and Grider set the stage. Addressed to the "officers on the Western waters" (west of the Blue Ridge), a letter said that if they did not "desist from their opposition to the British army, and take protection under his standard, he would march his army over the mountains, hang their leaders, and lay their country waste with fire and sword." The Patriot response changed the course of the Revolution in the South with the victory at King's Mountain.

In only one hour and five minutes, the American Patriots decimated Ferguson's American Tories, with every last one of them either dead or taken prisoner and Ferguson himself left dead on the battlefield—having signed his own death warrant with that inflammatory message sent just a month earlier.

In an address before the battle, Wrobel and Grider explain, Colonel Shelby encouraged his men to fight in frontier fashion:

> *Let each one of you be his own officer, taking every care you can of yourselves, and availing yourselves of every advantage that chance may throw in your way. If in the woods, shelter yourselves and give them Indian play! Advance from tree to tree, pressing the enemy and killing and disabling all you can.*

Isaac Shelby was given a major share of the credit for the victory and the turn toward success for the colonists. He instigated the campaign that led to King's Mountain, he drove it on and he shaped it. And it shaped him. Honor after honor—military prizes, towns and counties named after him, political appointments, elective office—were attracted like magnets to his sudden glory. Throughout his life, Isaac Shelby would point, again and again, to this battle as his defining moment. In his autobiography, he dismissed most awards, including two governorships, with few words. Instead, his most fervent expressions of gratitude were held for becoming "Old King's Mountain."

## SHAPING A NEW STATE

When Isaac Shelby came over the mountains into Kentucky with Daniel Boone and selected a homestead in 1776, he committed to Kentucky as his home. Although he would spend time throughout the South in the coming years, from that point on, Shelby considered himself—politically, economically, emotionally—a Kentuckian, even though no one would be called that for another decade.

December 1784 found delegates from each militia company in Danville for the first Kentucky Convention. Isaac Shelby was elected chairman. It would take ten applications to Virginia and the new United States for Kentucky to be admitted as the fifteenth state, but on Tuesday, May 15, 1792, the *Kentucky Gazette* reported:

> *The electors from the different counties in the State of Kentucky convened at Lexington agreeably to the Constitution, and proceeded to the election of a Governor and Senate. Isaac Shelby, Esq. was elected Governor.*

*Top*: Portrait of Isaac Shelby, first and fifth governor of Kentucky and the only sitting governor to lead troops into battle. Matthew Harris Jouett, artist. 1822. Reproduction 1903. *LOC 98510291.*

*Middle*: This copy of Governor Isaac Shelby's signature is from 1881. *Public domain. Courtesy of Wikimedia.*

*Bottom*: This sterling silver carving knife is engraved with Isaac Shelby's name. *Courtesy of the Arthur Francis collection.*

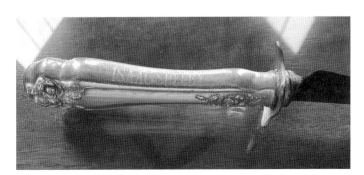

51

No one was surprised. Shelby's first term focused on securing Kentucky from Indian attacks and organizing its first government. French diplomats' rabble-rousing in Kentucky caused some trouble with what is known as the Citizen Genêt affair, but Shelby emerged unscathed. Shortly after that, President Washington announced a treaty with Spain that finally provided unrestricted use of the Mississippi River.

One of the final achievements of Shelby's first term, and a personal triumph, was the opening of an improved Wilderness Road. Since the day he crossed into Kentucky on Daniel Boone's Wilderness Trail, Shelby had lobbied for improved roads. When the state would not allocate funds, he persuaded more than one hundred citizens to pledge donations. As a result, in the coming years, the trail was widened and clearly marked and had an authorized militia dedicated to the protection of travelers, clearly opening up the new state to increased commerce and immigration.

## HOME AGAIN

With the state on sound financial footing with a well-organized judicial, military and government structure, Isaac Shelby gave himself over to private life. For the first time, Indian struggles were no longer a threat, and as he returned to Traveler's Rest, he vowed he was done with politics. He refused a second term as governor and subsequent requests that he run for the U.S. Senate. However, he did serve as an elector in national elections, voting for Thomas Jefferson in 1801 and 1805, James Madison in 1809 and James Monroe in 1812.

When Shelby returned home, he held more than six thousand acres in Lincoln, Fayette, Clark and Shelby Counties, much of it overseen by his sons. Slavery seemed necessary to Isaac. He was considered a kind master to the Traveler's Rest slaves, and it is thought that the "good master" in *Uncle Tom's Cabin* named Shelby is based on Isaac Shelby.

Cattle, pigs, mules, horses and sheep dotted Shelby's land. Plenty of grain, vegetables, tobacco and fruits were also produced, as well as hemp. Whiskey, as in other Kentucky areas, was one of the major productions. It required large corn and grain fields, but there were benefits, as the Shelby lands produced two thousand gallons of whiskey plus thousands of gallons of cider and apple brandy each year. Shelby liquor was prized in a state already becoming known around the world for fine whiskeys, deepening Kentucky's reliance on liquor as an item for export.

In 1811, at the ripe old age of sixty-one, Isaac Shelby had realized many youthful ambitions in a way of which few men can boast. He had a good name, a good conscience, a large and loving family and a home in which he could take pride. But Kentucky wasn't done with him yet.

## A SECOND TERM

Pressed into a second term as governor when the War of 1812 appeared imminent, Shelby reluctantly answered the call of his fellow Kentuckians. Within his first months as governor again, Shelby had only to post a call for volunteers and Kentuckians rushed in. Richard M. Johnson left Congress to raise five hundred mounted men and serve as aide to Northwest governor William Henry Harrison. In the first few months of Shelby's second governorship, more than seven thousand Kentuckians volunteered to fight. Many were turned away because the new state lacked weapons and supplies for them. Many went anyway. The state was filled with patriotism, rhetoric and ardor.

Harrison asked for troops to defend Fort Meigs, and Shelby sent 1,200 Kentuckians, among them his son, James. The fort held, but a company of Kentuckians was massacred in what is known as Dudley's Defeat. James Shelby was initially identified as killed in action but later turned up, having escaped capture.

Within a few weeks, troops were dragging home, out of provisions. Indians were setting fire to the prairies, turning what should have been forage for their horses into a raging weapon. Washington's leadership had put the cart before the horse, and Kentucky could not pay or appropriately provision its troops. Harrison and Shelby were frustrated and mortified with disappointment. Shelby put out a call to the state's wives, girlfriends and daughters for supplies, which were rushed to the front, despite weather and navigation delays.

On February 2, 1813, news of a victory at Frenchtown reached Frankfort, and much celebration broke out. Nearly everyone in the state had a son, brother, nephew or husband with Harrison; this was good news. But by eight o'clock that evening, the news was dire.

Orlando Brown, a small boy in the audience at a Frankfort theater, was watching the play and later related the following to historian Lewis Collins:

> *Governor Shelby and family were in the boxes, when an express, all bespattered with mud, made his appearance and whispered in the ear of the*

*Governor. He arose and left the house. Immediately the news spread to the audience that the detachment was cut to pieces. It was like a funeral wail that sob and then burst from every breast—for the flower of our youth was there, and that awful day "left many a sweet babe fatherless and many a widow mourning."*

When the Battle of River Raisin shook Shelby's faith in the course of the war being overseen in Washington, he vowed to engage and lead his own Kentucky Militia into the fray.

Shelby wrote to his friend Harrison about his anger and concerns, as quoted by Wrobel and Grider:

*My dear sir, of our success, is to depend on half measures such have been too often experienced during the last campaign nothing more be expected from Kentucky than what will be coerced by the laws of the land.*

*1. A Western Board of War should be named to reduce communication delays.*

*2. The United States must take command of the great lakes.*

*3. The militia must be paid promptly, out of necessity.*

*4. Our forces should be an imposing one.*

Later that year, Shelby himself led troops to battle at Monroviatown in retaliation for the two major massacres. The victory at the Battle of the Thames was the turning point for the Americans when Proctor's British regulars were resoundingly defeated and on the run and the Pan-Indian Confederacy leader lay dead on the battlefield.

After the war, Shelby declined President James Monroe's offer to become secretary of war. In his last act of public service, Shelby acted as commissioner, along with Andrew Jackson, to negotiate the Jackson Purchase from the Chickasaw Indian tribe.

Isaac Shelby died and is buried at his estate in Lincoln County. In 1952, 126 years after his death, Kentucky made the Shelby burial grounds a state historic site and restored the grounds. Kentucky had long before begun to bury all governors in Frankfort, but the family refused to have Isaac's body moved. So he rests with his family at the site he had chosen, loved and most valued, his Traveler's Rest.

Chapter 5

# HENRY CLAY AND
# THE WAR HAWKS

H enry Clay was born on April 12, 1777, at the Clay homestead in
Hanover County, Virginia. He was the seventh of nine children
born to the Reverend John Clay and Elizabeth (née Hudson) Clay
and the second son to be named Henry (the first died in infancy some years
previous). Clay was of entirely English and Virginian descent; his ancestor,
John Clay, settled in Virginia in 1613. From the seventeenth through the
nineteenth centuries, the Clay family became a well-known political family,
including three other U.S. senators, numerous state politicians and Clay's
cousin Cassius Clay, a prominent antislavery activist active in the mid-
nineteenth century.

## EARLY LIFE

Clay's childhood was difficult. His father was a Baptist preacher who
was poorly compensated for his efforts but had significant landholdings.
Unfortunately, Clay lost his father in 1781, plunging the family into financial
crisis. His mother later married Captain Henry Watkins, and the family
moved to Richmond, Kentucky, but Clay stayed behind, beginning a career
in law through a position in the office of the Virginia Court of Chancery.
He became the secretary to the chancellor, George Wythe, a noted scholar
and a professor of law. Wythe had a powerful effect on Clay's worldview,
with Clay embracing Wythe's belief that the example of the United States

could help spread human freedom around the world. Wythe subsequently arranged a position for Clay with Virginia attorney general Robert Brooke to study law. After completing his studies under Brooke, Clay was admitted to the Virginia bar in 1797.

## BUILDING A NAME AND A FARM

HENRY CLAY.

A young Henry Clay led the War Hawks. Philip Haas, engraver. 1844. *Courtesy of LOC 2013645246.*

In November 1797, Clay moved to Lexington, which was at that time a growing town in Kentucky. His license to practice law in Virginia enabled him to get his license to practice in Kentucky. Quickly, he earned a name for his legal skills as a member of the Democratic-Republican Party. However, many of his clients offered land, animals and slaves in lieu of money.

By 1804, Henry Clay began to acquire land for a farm for his wife, Lucretia Hart, and their young family. He had lived in Lexington since 1799, but by 1804, Clay was ready to move from his town home on Mill Street to a more substantial residence on the outskirts of town. By 1809, the center block of his new home was complete, and Clay was residing on the farm he named Ashland for the ash trees abundant on the property.

Henry Clay deeply loved Ashland—both the farm and home he had built on it. It provided a place of refuge and sanctuary from a difficult and often disappointing world and was one of the few places he regularly found happiness. The estate website highlights a sentiment Clay wrote on April 15, 1849:

*I am in one respect better off than Moses. He died in sight of, without reaching, the Promised Land. I occupy as good a farm as any that he would have found, if he had reached it; & it has been acquired not by hereditary descent, but by my own labor.*

Only the central section of Ashland, Henry Clay's estate, is original. The side sections were added later. *Author's collection.*

Henry Clay, the "Star of the West" and an important nineteenth-century political figure, began his law practice in this small brick building in downtown Lexington. *Author's collection.*

Henry Clay and Lucretia Hart Clay, photographed on their fiftieth wedding anniversary, probably in 1849. The original daguerreotype is in the Henry Clay Memorial Foundation papers, University of Kentucky. *Courtesy of Ashland, the Henry Clay Estate, Lexington, Kentucky.*

## BURR AND THE SPANISH CONSPIRACY

Henry Clay's defense of Aaron Burr for treason marked the start of his national political career—and the end of Burr's.

In the western portions of the new nation, Spain was flexing its muscle, aided by a surprising coconspirator. Aaron Burr, now frequently called "the Fallen Founding Father," was traveling Kentucky, drumming up support for a plan to cede Kentucky and the Louisiana Territory to Spain.

When Aaron Burr resigned the vice presidency a few days before his term expired on March 4, 1805, he faced murder charges in two states for killing Alexander Hamilton in a duel—an act that made him a target for the Federalists. He was a pariah in the East, hated even in his own Democratic-Republican Party, but westerners still appreciated him for his advocacy of western interests in the 1790s.

According to an article in *American Heritage*:

> *No one who met him ever forgot him. His charm captivated beautiful women, his eloquence moved the United States Senate to tears, his political skills carried him to the very threshold of the White House. Yet while still Vice President he was indicted for murder, and was already dreaming the dreams of empire that would bring him to trial for treason. After a century and a half, historians still cannot decide whether he was a traitor, a con man, or a mere adventurer.*

Henry Clay, then twenty-nine, was one of the prominent local figures Burr met for the first time in prosperous, cosmopolitan Lexington, Kentucky. In 1803, Clay became the representative of Fayette County in the Kentucky General Assembly, even though he was only twenty-six years old and could not legally stand for election. Clay was a rising star in the Kentucky legislature, already viewed by rich and poor as a good man and an outstanding lawyer, dealmaker and public speaker who was "going places."

Burr was arrested and charged with treason in Lexington, Kentucky, on December 6, 1806, and defended in his trial by Henry Clay. Released for lack of evidence, Burr headed south, supposedly to confer with the Spanish.

Federalists in Kentucky were a small but active, well-connected minority. For example, newspaper owner Humphrey Marshall and U.S. attorney Joseph "Jo" Daviess were both married to sisters of John Marshall, chief justice of the United States.

Aaron Burr shot Alexander Hamilton at Weehawken, on the banks of the Hudson, on July 11, 1804, hammering the final nail in the coffin of Burr's political career. Henry Davenport Northrop, artist. *Courtesy of LOC 2022633841.*

Marshall's newspaper accused Burr of starting conspiracies in Kentucky. Daviess sent a letter to President Jefferson saying Burr was assembling a plot to detach the western states and invade Mexico. As a result, President Jefferson issued a proclamation on November 27 calling for Burr's apprehension, again on charges of treason.

Burr hired Clay to defend him—again. At first, Clay declined to represent Burr at the next grand jury. The legislature had just elected him to fill an unexpired term in the U.S. Senate. Though he would only be a senator for three months, Clay was anxious to get there. But Clay's friends convinced him it would be dishonorable to abandon Burr.

When the grand jury met, Daviess asked for a postponement because his star witness could not get there. The judge granted Daviess's request for a second grand jury hearing.

At the second grand jury, Daviess asked for another postponement. Clay said another delay would persecute Burr, not prosecute him. The newspaper editors condemning Burr declared under oath that they had no objective evidence against him. Aaron Burr was prosecuted three times for treason and was acquitted each time, mainly due to Clay's defense tactics.

Henry Clay speaking during a Senate debate. Drawn by Peter F. Rothermel; engraved by Robert Whitechurch. 1850. *Courtesy of LOC 2014645186.*

As Clay traveled east to take his Senate seat, he saw that eastern Republicans, even President Jefferson, hated Burr as much as Federalists did. He began to wonder if Burr was guilty and if he had ruined his national political career before it started by defending him.

In Washington, President Jefferson showed Clay a letter he said was "positive proof" of Burr's treason. Clay was convinced Burr was guilty and never forgave Burr for lying to him.

## TO WASHINGTON

In 1806, while Clay was still legally underage, he was appointed to fill the United States Senate seat vacated by John Breckinridge's death. He was sworn in on December 29, 1806, the term ended in three months and he returned to Kentucky at the beginning of 1807.

On his return to Kentucky, Clay was elected Speaker of the Kentucky House of Representatives. During that time, suits for aristocrats were made from broadcloth made in Britain. On January 3, 1809, Clay introduced a resolution requiring members to come in homespun suits to boycott British goods. Only two members voted against the resolution. This action foretold Clay's activism toward creating recognition of his fledgling nation.

In 1810, Clay was sent to the Senate for a second time to fill out the seat vacated by Senator Buckner Thruston. But his return home would be brief.

In 1811, Henry Clay was elected to the United States House of Representatives and was chosen as Speaker of the House. At thirty-four, he was the youngest person to become Speaker, a distinction he held until the election of thirty-year-old Robert M.T. Hunter in 1839.

As quoted on the Constitution Center's website, addressing his fellow lawmakers soon after he was first elected Speaker, Clay said:

> *I am sensible of the imperfections which I bring along with me, and a consciousness of these would deter me from attempting a discharge of the duties of the chair, did I not rely confidently upon your support. Should the rare and delicate occasion present itself when your speaker should be called upon to check or control the wanderings or intemperances in debate, your justice will, I hope, ascribe to his interposition the motives only of public good and a regard to the dignity of the house.*

Immediately, Clay took action to form different committees, carefully filling them with like-minded men. In short order, he had not only gained control of the house but also made the position of Speaker one of political force, second only that of the president. He remained in the post until 1814.

Clay was exceptional in his ability to control the legislative agenda through well-placed allies and the establishment of new committees and departed from precedent by frequently taking part in floor debates. He gained the nickname "the Great Compromiser" as a vigorous and persuasive speaker while in the House. Yet he also earned a reputation for personal courteousness and fairness in his rulings and committee appointments. Clay's drive to increase the power of the office of Speaker was aided by President James Madison, who deferred to Congress in most matters.

## WAR HAWKS

During this time, Clay became one of the leaders of the faction called the War Hawks: young, anti-British members of Congress primarily from the South and West who, like Clay, supported going to war with Great Britain to force recognition of the United States' legitimacy. Although they were young and even called "the boys" in Congress, the War Hawks gained influence given the leadership and charisma of Henry Clay. Buoyed by the support of fellow War Hawks, Clay was elected Speaker of the House for the Twelfth Congress. It was to be a busy session.

Clay's role as a champion of American industry and agriculture is symbolized by the anvil and spindle, the plough and cows in the fields and the ship. John Sartain, engraver, from John Neagle's portrait. *Courtesy of LOC 2003690763.*

The name War Hawks was created informally by Congressman John Randolph, who opposed entry into the war. Because it wasn't an official designation, there was never a roster of who was and who wasn't a War Hawk, although Speaker of the House Henry Clay was certainly considered their leader. Members of Congress from northeastern states disagreed with the War Hawks. They did not want to wage war against Great Britain because they believed their coastal states would bear the physical and economic consequences of an attack by the British fleet more than southern or western states would.

On November 4, 1811, President Madison (who had been negotiating with the British for years as secretary of state about allowing America to trade freely as a neutral nation in the British-French War) called the Twelfth Congress into special session. His message to Congress recommended that provisions be made for the United States to prepare for war. Among these provisions was a bill to increase the regular army from ten thousand to twenty-five thousand and a bill to provide for a volunteer force of fifty thousand men. On April 1, 1812, Congress passed an embargo act as a forerunner to the actual declaration of war.

While Henry Clay's War Hawks and the rest of the Twelfth Congress, with President Madison, debated the question of war, the British minister and Monroe continued negotiations concerning impressment and repeal of the British Orders in Council. The United States had a similar grievance against France over trade impediments, which would have justified going to war with that country and Great Britain both. Still, British policy caused so much more suffering in the United States than did French that Clay and the other War Hawks convinced their cohorts to move forward with the decision to declare war against Britain alone.

The War Hawks cited multiple sources of tension between the two nineteenth-century powerhouses as arguments for war—including violations by the British of U.S. maritime rights, the effects of the Napoleonic Wars and lingering animosity from the Revolutionary War. In addition, the impressment of American sailors to serve on British ships was a concern of the eastern colonies. Still, inland Kentucky objected to blockades by Britain and impressment only on the grounds of national pride.

On April 14, 1812, a letter by Henry Clay appeared in the *Washington Intelligencer*:

> *Let war therefore be forthwith proclaimed against England. With her there can be no motive for delay. Any further discussion, any new attempt at negotiation, would be as fruitless as it would be dishonorable.*

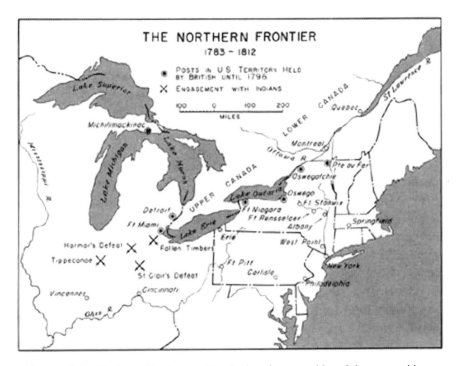

This map of the Northwest Territory and battle sites gives some idea of the geographic scope where Kentuckians fought. *Courtesy of Wikimedia.*

At the same time, the western frontier was feeling pressure from Indigenous peoples, who were allying to stop the encroachment of White settlers. The War Hawks believed the British were financing Indigenous tribes in their resistance, which only galvanized them to declare war against Great Britain. As the War Hawks represented states in the South and West, this was a critical issue for them and their constituents. Henry Clay and South Carolina's John Calhoun led in putting forth their demands:

- Cease all naval impressments and British-Canadian support of Indian attacks.
- Restore national honor.
- Acquire new territory in Canada and Florida.
- Remove European powers from our borders and deprive Indians of weapons.

In addition, Clay and other War Hawks also demanded that the British revoke the Orders in Council, a series of decrees that had resulted in what amounted to a commercial war with the United States. These ordered a blockade of French and allied ports, essentially stopping trade with the United States. This order also required all ships coming into English ports to be checked for military supplies that could have aided France. Ships that did not stop to be checked at English ports were subject to British seizure. Though Clay recognized the dangers inherent in fighting Britain, one of the most powerful countries in the world, he saw it as the only realistic alternative to a humiliating submission to British attacks on American shipping and the end of expansion in the West.

Interestingly, the British had already conceded to this demand, but slow communication hindered the American response. Finally, on June 16, 1812, two days before the United States' declaration of war, the British secretary of state for foreign affairs announced in Parliament that the Orders in Council would be suspended. Might the War of 1812 have been avoided if we'd had texting then?

## MADISON'S WAR

A bill declaring war, written by William Pinkney, U.S. attorney general, was introduced into the House of Representatives by War Hawk John Calhoun. After a lengthy debate the following day, the bill passed the House by a vote of seventy-nine to forty-nine.

In the Senate, the measure was discussed in a secret session for several days and finally passed as a slightly amended bill on June 17 with a vote of nineteen for and thirteen against, a relatively small margin. Like today, the voices in both houses represented almost precisely party division: agricultural states of the West and South favored the war, while the commercial states of the North, particularly the eastern ones, voted against. The bill passed the House as amended by the Senate, and on June 18, it was sent to the president.

Madison signed the declaration of war on June 18, 1812, beginning the War of 1812. Forty-one days after the United States Congress declared war, the news reached London, on July 29, 1812. Two days later, the British ministry ordered its first countermeasures. It forbade British ships to sail except in convoys and restrained American vessels in British ports. The Orders in Council had been repealed on June 23, 1812, but the ministers did not intend to take additional measures until they could learn the American reaction. Word of the repeal of the Orders did not reach President James

Madison until August 12, some fifty days later. Even then, Madison refused to halt hostilities because he did not know how Britain was reacting to the American declaration of war.

Things were heating up in Washington. Clay and Calhoun, both Democrat-Republicans, had fought with the Federalists for nearly a decade over war with Britain or France. The Federalists, primarily composed of New England states, felt the South and West were going to war against the more commercial, and therefore wealthier, states. The debate continued to rage throughout the war, so that the United States, in one way, was at war with itself as well as England.

Hoping Great Britain would sooner meet demands than go to war again, Secretary of State Monroe, soon after the declaration of war was proclaimed, empowered Jonathan Russell, an ambassador in London, to arrange an armistice between the parties. The critical conditions were that the Orders in Council be repealed and Great Britain immediately discontinue the practice of impressment of seamen from American vessels, together with restoration of those already impressed.

In London, British secretary of state Lord Castlereagh was having none of it. He utterly rejected the proposal, refused to meet with Russell and claimed Russell had no authority to propose or participate in diplomatic relations between Great Britain and America. And so the War of 1812 began in earnest.

Throughout the war, Clay frequently communicated with Secretary of State James Monroe and Secretary of War William Eustis, even though he advocated for the latter's replacement. Proposals for mediation were repeatedly sent to the British, and London summarily rejected each.

Initially, the war went poorly for the Americans, and Clay lost many friends and relatives in the fighting. According to the Kentucky National Guard Museum website, of the approximately twenty-five thousand Kentuckians who served during the war, over six thousand were killed in battle, and nearly seventeen thousand succumbed to illness. Of the Americans killed in the War of 1812, 66 percent were Kentuckians. Four of every five military-age male Kentuckians served during the war. And even after the war had officially ended, the backwoods hunters of Kentucky and Tennessee took pride in defeating the professional British army at the Battle of New Orleans in 1815.

# A Useful Life

Clay, after helping to negotiate the Treaty of Ghent, ending the War of 1812, returned to the United States in September 1815. Despite his absence, he was elected to another term in the House of Representatives. On his return to Congress, Clay again won election as Speaker of the House. The War of 1812 strengthened Clay's support for interventionist economic policies, such as federally funded internal improvements, which he believed were necessary to enhance the country's infrastructure system. He embraced President Madison's ambitious domestic package, which included infrastructure investment, tariffs to protect domestic manufacturing and spending increases for the army and navy. With the help of John C. Calhoun and William Lowndes, Clay passed the Tariff of 1816, which served the dual purpose of raising revenue and protecting American manufacturing.

Between 1810 and 1824, Clay was elected to seven terms in the House. Elected Speaker six times, Clay's cumulative tenure in office of 10 years, 196 days, is the second longest, surpassed to date only by twentieth-century Texan Sam Rayburn.

Clay served at almost every level of government possible in the nineteenth century: the Kentucky State House of Representatives, the United States Senate, the United States House of Representatives and the executive branch, as secretary of state. On top of that, he ran for president three times over three decades on three different party tickets (the Democratic-Republican

A mural on the side of the U.S. post office in Portsmouth, Ohio, depicts Henry Clay showing off his oratorial skills. Clarence Holbrook Carter, artist. 1937. *Courtesy of Wikimedia.*

Party in 1824, the National Republican Party in 1832 and the Whig Party in 1844). Decades later, President Abraham Lincoln declared Henry Clay his "beau ideal" and modeled many of his policies on Clay's ideals.

Clay's beloved Ashland is preserved as a museum and historical shrine, surrounded by parklike grounds filled with sculptures and trees.

Chapter 6

# TECUMSEH AND TENSKWATAWA

Without a doubt, Tecumseh—also spelled Tecumthe, Tikamthe or Tecumtha—is one of the most famous Indigenous leaders in history and a man who helped repel the American invasion of Canada during the War of 1812. His name was Tecumseh, and his impact on Canadian and United States history would be massive.

## EARLY LIFE

Born to Shawnee parents Pukeshinwau and Methoataaskee around 1768 near Chillicothe, Ohio, and given a name that means Shooting Star or I Cross the Way, Tecumseh would enter the world during a time of transition for his people. Pukeshinwau was a Shawnee chief, and Tecumseh was surrounded by highly regarded siblings, including triplet brothers. One triplet, Sauwaseekau, was killed at the Battle of Fallen Timbers; the second, Kumskaukau, may have died young, for no records exist of his life; and the third, who would eventually be known as Tenskwatawa, was a fussy baby who was given the name Lalawethika, He Makes a Loud Noise. Later in life, he would be known as the Shawnee Prophet.

From the ages of six to fourteen, Tecumseh saw the American military becoming more aggressive, leading to the death of Tecumseh's father on October 10, 1774, during a confrontation at Point Pleasant in northern

*Left*: An 1868 portrait of Tecumseh by Benson John Lossing, after an 1808 pencil sketch by Pierre Le Dru. *Courtesy of Wikimedia.*

*Right*: Tenskwatawa, the Prophet, worked beside (and occasionally thwarted) his brother Tecumseh's Pan-Indian Confederacy. Thomas Loraine McKenney & James Hall, authors. *History of the Indian Tribes of North America. Courtesy of Wikimedia.*

Ohio. When his mother went to Missouri, Tecumseh and his siblings were left in the care of Tecumapease, their older sister. She taught Tecumseh their culture, while his brother Cheeseekau taught him to be a warrior. Of her brothers, Tecumapease was closest to Tecumseh.

Three years later, the Shawnee community split, and Tecumseh moved to the Great Miami River, a tributary of the Ohio River in southwest Ohio. By this point, Tecumseh, now nineteen, had seen his father killed by Americans, the tribes' villages destroyed by settlers and their land seized. It fostered in him a deep hatred of Americans, which would lead him to become an ally of Britain and Canada.

For the next several years, Tecumseh led skirmishes of Shawnee warriors against the Americans, during which time his elder brother Cheeseekau was killed. In one attack, Tecumseh's scouting party aided in the American defeat at the Battle of Wabash in southern Indiana. But despite his hatred of Americans, Tecumseh pushed back against cruelty for cruelty's sake. During a raid, he saw an American tied to a stake and burned. He let loose a tirade of anger at his fellow warriors, insisting that they never torture a prisoner in his presence again. It was a policy he upheld until his death.

In 1791, he took part as a minor war chief in the Northwest Indian War. There, he saw how an Indigenous confederacy might come together to fight the war as the Northwest Tribes advocated, inspiring him later to form his own confederacy.

But on August 20, 1794, the hope of that initial Indigenous confederacy to keep the Americans off their land was dashed when the Americans decisively won the Battle of Fallen Timbers. Again, Tecumseh distinguished himself as a warrior, but the Treaty of Greenville brought fighting to an end. Tecumseh and other Native Americans felt that land could not be owned but was shared by all peoples and could not be negotiated away. He fought the treaty but didn't have enough power to sway anyone.

In an 1810 message to President James Madison, Tecumseh wrote,

> *These lands are ours. No one has a right to remove us, because we were the first owners. The Great Spirit above has appointed this place for us, on which to light our fires and here we will remain. As to boundaries, the Great Spirit above knows no boundaries, nor will his red people acknowledge any.*

By 1800, Tecumseh was thirty-two years old and he had seen his people's land disappear, their livelihood heavily disrupted and diseases like smallpox rage through the land, ravaging Indigenous populations. He was ready to fight back.

## BECOMING A WARRIOR LEADER

The path for Tecumseh to come to Canada and join Great Britain against the United States would begin with his brother Tenskwatawa, who in 1805 had a dream that transformed his philosophy overnight. Tenskwatawa began to preach, adopting the name the Prophet and speaking against alcohol, slander and the loss of ancestral traditions. He especially hated the Americans, calling them the scum of the great water. Tecumseh was inspired by his brother's teachings and changed his habits, eating only Indigenous food, wearing traditional Shawnee clothing and never drinking alcohol. And he saw his brother's philosophies as an opportunity to harness the energy of this movement toward retaining Indigenous land. In the book *Tecumseh and the Prophet*, Tecumseh's resilience is evident in this quote:

*Show respect to all people, but grovel to none. When you rise in the morning, give thanks for the light, for your life, for your strength. Give thanks for your food and for the joy of living. If you find no reason to give thanks, the fault lies within yourself.*

At the same time his brother was spreading the message of a return to Indigenous culture, the possibility of war between Britain and America was increasing. With tensions mounting, Tecumseh moved his people toward where Tippecanoe is today. A village of two hundred houses was built and named Prophetstown for his brother, the cultural touchpoint for their community. At its height, it is believed that six thousand people settled around it, making it larger than any American city in the area at the time.

In 1808, Tenskwatawa was invited to Upper Canada to preach but was unable to go. In his place, Tecumseh arrived on June 8. The event raised Tecumseh's profile among the Native Americans, Canadians and British.

While Tecumseh was away, the Americans conducted a vast land grab under the Treaty of Fort Wayne. Furious, Tecumseh told the British he was ready for war. It also increased his desire to create an Indigenous confederacy. In 1809, nearly 1,400 Potawatomi, Delaware, Miami and Eel River Indians and their allies witnessed the Treaty of Fort Wayne, ceding two and a half million acres of tribal lands in present-day Michigan, Indiana, Illinois and Ohio in exchange for a peace that would not last.

The great war chief Tecumseh and his brother spent the decades before 1812 mobilizing a new and more inclusive Pan-Indian Confederacy that would stand together and repulse the hordes of White settlers encroaching on Indian land. While they were only partially successful in creating an actual pan-Indian pact, enough Indigenous nations banded together that with British aid, they stood a good chance of ending western migration in the United States.

Tecumseh spent large parts of 1809–11 traveling to the Mississippi River, down the Illinois River, up to present-day Wisconsin, then into Tennessee and Missouri, advocating for the confederacy. He reached the Gulf of Mexico and traveled up to the northern Red River with the aim of creating an Indigenous nation that would stretch between the Mississippi and the Rockies.

Two events would aid Tecumseh that year. In 1811, the New Madrid Earthquake and the Great Comet of 1811 occurred—which were taken as signs by most Natives, meaning that the Tecumseh and his Pan-Indian Confederacy should be supported. The Prophet, Tenskwatawa, had predicted both.

*Meeting of Brock and Tecumseh, 1812* by Charles William Jefferys (1915) depicts Tecumseh and General Sir Isaac Brock meeting in the War of 1812. *Courtesy of Wikimedia.*

Americans, however, saw Tecumseh's organizing as a portent of attack. As governor of Ohio, William Henry Harrison, who would become the shortest-serving American president in history, organized a meeting with Tecumseh in July 1811. Tecumseh would arrive with three hundred warriors; some accounts say it was more than four hundred. At the meeting, Tecumseh was supported by notable Indigenous leaders like Blue Jacket and Roundhead, and he told the governor his only aim for the confederacy was peace. Satisfied, Harrison dismissed his militia, but settlers still believed that Native American organization could only mean war.

According to legend, Tecumseh was given a chair at that meeting and told by officers that his father—meaning Governor Harrison—offered him a seat. According to Cozzens, Tecumseh allegedly responded: "My father. The sun is my father, and the earth is my mother. She gives me nourishment and I will rest on her bosom."

After the meeting, Cozzens writes, Harrison said of Tecumseh:

> *If it were not for the vicinity of the United States, Tecumseh would perhaps be the founder of an empire that would rival in glory Mexico or Peru. No difficulties deter him. For four years he has been in constant motion. You see him today on the Wabash and in a short time hear of him on the shores of Lake Erie or Michigan, or on the banks of the Mississippi and wherever he goes he makes an impression favorable to his service. He is now upon the last round to put a finishing stroke upon his work.*

But in this meeting, Tecumseh made a momentous mistake when he told Harrison that he would be leaving with fifty warriors for the south in August and would be gone until spring. Before he left, Tecumseh told his brother to wait to engage the Americans until the confederacy was stronger. But Harrison's troops marched to Prophetstown and encamped nearby. The Prophet saw a threat and an opportunity to demonstrate his power.

## An Uneasy Alliance

When Tenskwatawa and a band of his warriors attacked Harrison's troops at dawn on November 7, 1811, the Battle of Tippecanoe led to a devastating defeat for the Prophet. After the battle, Harrison and his men entered the Native village, found it empty and burned it and the food supplies. The victory attached the nickname Tippecanoe to Harrison, who

A small group of dragoons under the command of Major Joseph H. Daviess fight Natives during the battle of Tippecanoe. *Courtesy of LOC 2003668276.*

would use the "Tippecanoe and Tyler, too" slogan to become president three decades later.

Tecumseh was furious with his brother for the attack. His brother's tirade at Tenskwatawa for insubordination and lack of proficiency as a warrior caused Tenskwatawa to flee to Canada. The defeat convinced many Indians in the Northwest Territory that they needed British support to prevent American settlers from pushing them further west, out of their lands. A tenuous and shaky alliance formed. Tecumseh's Pan-Indian Confederacy was happening.

When war finally came, Tecumseh and 350 warriors from various tribes went immediately to Canada, where the British were strengthening their defenses. The British recognized Tecumseh as the most influential of their Indigenous allies and relied on him to direct warrior forces.

On July 25, 1812, American major James Denny marched 120 Ohio volunteers near the camp of Tecumseh, who organized an ambush that routed the Americans, leading to the first American casualties of the War of 1812. This victory and similar early attacks had a devastating impact on the confidence of General William Hull, who had brought his American forces into the area in July. During one of these raids, Tecumseh suffered a wound to his neck but recovered quickly.

John Richardson, a soldier and the first Canadian-born author to achieve international recognition, met Tecumseh on August 9, and Cozzens relates that he described him as a man with "that ardor of expression in his eye, that could not fail to endear him to the soldier hearts of those who stood around him."

In a decisive coordinated effort, Tecumseh and Chief Roundhead, leading hundreds of canoes and 530 warriors, landed near Detroit. The British followed the next day. The British openly marched toward Detroit, while Tecumseh and his men went north through the forest. Already in an agitated state, General Hull feared there were thousands of warriors in the woods. Tecumseh shifted his men throughout the trees, making it seem like the trees were full of Indigenous warriors. As the British shelled the fort, General Hull surrendered Detroit without a single shot from the Americans.

The loss of Fort Detroit was a national disgrace for the Americans, and General Hull would be court-martialed, convicted and sentenced to death before he was pardoned by President James Madison.

British general Isaac Brock wrote to Prime Minister Lord Liverpool:

*He who attracted most of my attention was a Shawnee chief, Tecumseh, brother to The Prophet, who for the last two years has carried on, contrary to our remonstrances, an active warfare against the United States. A more sagacious or more gallant warrior does not I believe exist. He was the admiration of everyone who conversed with him.*

Through all of this, Tecumseh's primary focus was to create a peaceful and permanent nation for his people rather than to defend Canada from the Americans. Brock assured Tecumseh that the British supported the Indigenous land claims. He even wrote to his superiors stating that the restoration of land taken from the Native Americans should be part of any peace treaty.

Harrison would also say of Tecumseh:

*The implicit obedience and respect which the followers of Tecumseh pay to him is really astonishing, and more than any other circumstances bespeaks him one of those uncommon geniuses which spring up occasionally to produce revolutions and overturn the order of things.*

But he would call Tecumseh's brother "a fool, who speaks not the words of the Great Spirit but those of the devil, and of the British agents," according to Cozzens.

## DUDLEY'S DEFEAT AND MASSACRE

Throughout 1812 and 1813, battles raged both on the northwestern front and in the waters off the East Coast of the United States of America, engaging Native, British, Canadian and American combatants. In the northwest, Tecumseh marshaled Natives to join his Pan-Indian Confederacy to push back against White settlement. By April 1813, after the massacre at the River Raisin and other losses, Harrison was desperate to regain lost ground in Michigan and prevent the British from moving into Ohio.

Toward the end of April 1813, Tecumseh and Roundhead led a force of 1,200 warriors to the recently constructed Fort Meigs. The fort was under the command of William Henry Harrison, who thought it best to conduct the battle from within the fort. Historian Allan Eckert relates that Tecumseh sent Harrison this note:

> *I have with me 800 braves. You have an equal number in your hiding place. Come out with them and give me battle. You talked like a brave when we met at Vincennes and I respected you, but now you hide behind logs and in the earth like a groundhog. Give me your answer.*

Entrenched at Fort Meigs with troops whose enlistments were expiring, Harrison called on Governor Isaac Shelby for support, who sent a cousin, Green Clay, and his son James Shelby. Harrison's plan called for eight hundred of Clay's men to land on the British side, a mile west of the British batteries on the heights. The Kentucky force was to get behind and flank the battery positions and spike the British guns with metal stakes.

Reenactors prepare to battle at the two hundredth anniversary of the Battle of the River Raisin in Michigan. Dana Stiefel. *Courtesy of River Raisin National Battlefield Park, NPS.gov.*

Tecumseh's strong sense of fairness is depicted in this picture, which may reflect his anger at the savagery at Fort Meigs. Virtue, Emma's & Co., publisher. 1860. *Courtesy of LOC 2012645310.*

Colonel William Dudley, with 846 Kentucky troops in twelve boats, veered toward the north bank, while Clay led his remaining Kentuckians to land on the south side and engage the Indians on his way to Fort Meigs. Unwilling to wait for the spikes to be sent from Fort Meigs, Dudley's men used broken musket ramrods and anything else at hand to plug the firing holes of the cannons. Emboldened by success, the Kentuckians chased the British, scattering themselves widely throughout the woods to within sight of the British and Indian camp.

Tecumseh's warriors raised the alarm and soon had the scattered militiamen surrounded. Dudley lay dead, and the only thing that prevented another massacre was the British taking the prisoners to the camp. But enraged Indians forced the prisoners to run the gauntlet through two lines of braves who struck them with tomahawks, clubs and pistol butts. As a result, more than twenty militiamen were killed and scalped, and all the Americans might have been slaughtered had Tecumseh not intervened, shouting angrily: "Are there no men here?"

Tecumseh rushed in to stop the killing. After his death, such actions would give Tecumseh the image of a noble and merciful warrior.

The Native Americans and British inflicted heavy casualties on the Americans, but they could not capture the fort, and the siege of the fort was eventually lifted.

Tecumseh was engaged with his warriors during both sieges at Fort Meigs. His disgust at the lack of oversight, indeed the support of drunkenness and violence among Natives, began to foment his distrust of the British. But his options were diminishing.

Tecumseh was not present at the Battle of River Raisin at Frenchtown, which may help account for the savage butchery of the Kentuckians that ensued. Word of this massacre, on top of Dudley's Defeat, would enrage the Americans—and bring the full force of the "Kaintucks" to bear on October 5, 1813, at Moraviantown.

## LOSS OF A GREAT WARRIOR-STATESMAN

The Battle of the Thames was a devastating defeat for the British, with 634 men killed or captured. But the most significant loss by far was that of Tecumseh. For several days, rumors swirled that Tecumseh was only wounded and would again lead his people. But, sadly, this was not the case.

As for who killed Tecumseh, that is up for debate. Richard Mentor Johnson is said to have been the man who killed Tecumseh, although he never confirmed this, stating only that he killed a tall, good-looking Indian in a headdress. However, even without confirming it, he would use the rumors to his political advantage and be known as the Man Who Killed Tecumseh. As he ran for the U.S. Senate, his supporters chanted: "Rumpsey dumpsey, rumpsey dumpsey, Johnson killed Tecumseh."

Johnson was elected to the Senate in 1836 and eventually became vice president of the United States. Another man, David King, was also named as possibly killing Tecumseh, and many eyewitnesses claimed it was William Whitley during the Forlorn Hope charge. Several others claimed to have brought the great warrior down. We will never know.

Eyewitnesses reported many Americans desecrating the Indigenous dead by taking off strips of skin and removing scalps. Kentucky frontiersman Simon Kenton, who had met Tecumseh on several occasions, was asked to identify Tecumseh's body, but when he saw the mutilation taking place, Kenton later said he had purposefully misidentified Roundhead as Tecumseh. On other occasions, he told of picking a random Indian corpse, not Roundhead. Kenton likely did this to allow the Native warriors to locate and remove Tecumseh's body to avoid desecration.

Tecumseh urges on his Native brothers as the Kentucky militia surge into the swamp.
*Courtesy of Wikimedia Commons.*

Tecumseh's burial site is unknown, and it is believed his warriors took his body and buried it far from the battlefield. Stories told by the warriors at the battle vary. Some say that fellow warriors were forced to leave his body on the field (Native custom required Indigenous dead be removed during retreat); others said he was carried off, possibly mortally wounded. There are also stories of Canadians taking his body and burying it in Sandwich, Upper Canada.

The death of Tecumseh was not only the loss of a critical ally for the British, but it was also the end of any hope of an Indigenous confederacy. According to author Peter Cozzens, Odawa Chief Naywash said, "Since our Great Chief Tecumseh has been killed, we do not listen to one another, we do not rise together."

A week after his death, the tribes who participated in the battle signed a truce with the Americans. The British tried to bring them back into the war, but all these attempts failed. The Kentucky men who rode down Tecumseh and killed him were very aware of the danger to the fledgling nation that he presented in gathering Natives together. Never again would Natives hold power against America, even as America spread west, reducing Native territory further.

## TECUMSEH'S LEGACY

Today, Tecumseh is arguably one of North America's most honored Indigenous leaders. His life is recorded in thousands of books written about his life and times. He became a folk hero in Canadian and Indigenous history, and many call him a hero who transcends cultural identity. In Canada, Tecumseh is honored as a hero of Canada for his defense of the country during the War of 1812. In a ranking of the greatest Canadians by the Canadian Broadcasting Corporation in 2004, Tecumseh placed thirty-fourth. The HMCS Tecumseh naval reserve in Calgary is named for him, and a commemorative two-dollar coin was released to honor him on June 18, 2012. In the United States, battleships, parks, towns, schools, companies and products bear his name—from car parts to refrigeration. In Chillicothe, Ohio, the outdoor drama *Tecumseh* plays throughout each summer.

Babies were named after him, in a few cases becoming as famous as their namesake. According to Wikipedia's list of memorials to Tecumseh, Union Civil War general William Tecumseh Sherman was named Tecumseh because "my father…had caught a fancy for the great chief of the Shawnees." Evolutionary biologist and cognitive scientist W. Tecumseh

Actually Tamanend, chief of the Delawares, this statue at the U.S. Naval Academy is now commonly called Tecumseh by students and the community. *Courtesy of Wikimedia.*

Fitch was actually named after the general, not after Tecumseh. Another Civil War general, Napoleon Jackson Tecumseh Dana, also bore the name of the Shawnee leader.

A Tecumseh statue at the U.S. Naval Academy provides a living symbol of military might. Each year, the statue is painted before finals and football games or when America goes to war as a reflection of the fighting spirit. Actually, the statue is a bronze replica of the figurehead of USS *Delaware* representing the peacemaker Tamanend. Midshipmen simply preferred the warrior Tecumseh, so they started calling the statue Tecumseh. The original figurehead was rescued after the vessel was sunk and displayed at the United States Naval Academy (hence the naval connection). It stands in front of the courtyard of Bancroft Hall (the academy's dormitory), lending the name Tecumseh Court or simply T Court to the area around it.

Supposedly, the great leader found a way, after death, to strike back at Americans. Tecumseh's foe and Tippecanoe hero President William Henry Harrison's death from pneumonia on April 4, 1841, was the first in a series of tragedies that struck presidents winning an election at the start of a new decade—a pattern that would become known as Tecumseh's Curse or the Curse of Tippecanoe. Other unfortunate presidents elected at the beginning of decades were: Abraham Lincoln, first elected in 1860; James Garfield, elected in 1880; William McKinley, elected to his second term in 1900; Warren G. Harding, elected in 1920; Franklin Roosevelt, elected to his third term in 1940; and John F. Kennedy, elected in 1960. Some hypothesize that the curse is now broken. Reagan was the first to foil Tecumseh's Curse when he was shot by John Hinkley but survived. George W. Bush, elected in 2000, survived two assassination attempts and foiled several alleged plots during his two terms. Since Richard Nixon, every president has been targeted with at least one assassination plot, but none have died. Perhaps Tecumseh's revenge has been satisfied.

British soldier in the War of 1812 John Richardson wrote a poem called "Tecumseh" or "The Warrior of the West" to preserve the image and name of the man he greatly admired. At age sixteen, Richardson enlisted in the British Forty-First Regiment of Foot. During his service with this regiment, he met Chief Tecumseh and Major General Isaac Brock, whom he later wrote about in his novel *The Canadian Brothers*. While stationed at Fort Malden during the War of 1812, Richardson witnessed the execution of an American prisoner by Tecumseh's forces at the River Raisin. This traumatic experience haunted him for the rest of his life. During the War of 1812, Richardson was imprisoned for a year in Kentucky after his capture during the Battle of Moraviantown.

Within thirty-five years of Tecumseh's death at Moraviantown, most Native nations east of the Mississippi River had been forcibly relocated.

Chapter 7

# WOMEN AND SLAVES
# IN THE WAR OF 1812

W hile the War of 1812 is considered a conflict between men, Kentucky women and enslaved people knew that it was their fight, too. Kentucky was a slave state but had strong abolitionist segments, and Kentucky soldiers frequently brought their wives or enslaved people along. Children often came along, too, and some were born during the war.

An accurate account of the War of 1812 must also include stories of those affected by the absence of fathers, husbands or sons in service to their country. But unfortunately, it is the voices of the mothers, wives, daughters and slaves of the War of 1812 that are often unheard and unrecorded. But there are a few.

## SOLDIER SLAVES

Many enslaved people were forced by their masters to go to war, but even then, some of the enslaved went willingly to protect their own families and homes. George and Richard were two enslaved men listed among the *Kentucky Soldiers of the War of 1812*, compiled by M.S. Wilder. Their rank is listed as "servant," with the enlistment date of February 8, 1815, to March 7, 1815. The men are listed under the heading: "Roll of Field and Staff, Francisco's Regiment of Kentucky Militia, War of 1812—Commanded by Lieutenant-Colonel John Francisco."

It is doubtful that these and other such men provided service only to their owners. Likely they moved heavy artillery, reloaded in the line of fire and fought hand-to-hand throughout the battle engagements and skirmishes. Moreover, they (and their wives and children) endangered themselves when they brought water, ammunition, weapons and food to militiamen during battle.

In the midst of the War of 1812, a proclamation promised freedom to enslaved people who deserted to the British, according to an article on History.com. This proclamation resulted in what has been called "one of the most extraordinarily effective mass military emancipations ever seen in the United States." Thousands of the enslaved are reported to have gained freedom by supporting the British, the largest emancipation before the Civil War. Admiral George Cockburn's Colonial Marines, for example, helped in the burning of Washington, D.C. On the other side, an estimated 330 soldier-slaves in the Battalions of Free Men of Color fought for the Americans in the Battle of New Orleans, many of whom may have been freed precisely because they chose to fight for the United States.

## WOMEN IN THE CAMPS

Unwilling to abandon their husbands, wives, girlfriends and daughters generally went willingly to war with them. They served as camp followers to nurse, feed, clean and support their men and troops at large. In camps, they were seamstresses, laundresses and companions to the soldiers, but not every soldier could bring his family along. Chosen by a lottery system, only six wives were allowed in each camp for every one hundred soldiers. As a rule, the lottery was held the evening before leaving to allow the benefit of hope as long as possible. Tickets marked "to go" or "not to go" were placed in a hat. Each woman then walked past, drawing her fate in front of the eyes of the entire company. If a woman's husband was killed, she had three to six months to grieve, and then she had to remarry or leave the camp (with children), no matter how far from home.

Abigail Adams, wife of John, regarded the coming of the War of 1812 as the realization of what she had long foreseen. She had lived through the Revolutionary War and never wavered in her opposition to British rule of the American colonies. Through that conflict, she managed the family farm and raised children while assuring her absent husband that she was coping well. "I would not have you distressed about me, danger, they say, makes people valiant."

Her experiences and position as former first lady in a new country allowed her to serve as a role model to women nationwide. And she was hardly quiet

*Left*: A woman considers her plight on the battlefield at the two hundredth anniversary reenactment of the Battle of the River Raisin. David Kaszubski. *Courtesy of River Raisin National Battlefield Park, NPS.gov.*

*Right*: Guides at the Fort Meigs State Memorial prepare to give a tour of the facility on a clear day in the summer. *National Register of Historic Places. Courtesy of Wikimedia.*

about giving women their just due, both to her husband and others. Author Robert Barr quotes her thus, "If we mean to have heroes, statesmen, and philosophers, we should have learned women."

Before the Revolution, the role of nurse was a male-dominated one. But when men were needed on the battlefield, women were enlisted as nurses for battlefield hospitals, and the role of women in nursing exploded, both on battlefields and in hospitals. And serving in military hospitals was one source of income. Women acted as nurses, attendants, wardmasters or cleaners. According to *In the Midst of Alarms*, they were paid at most six dollars per month and one ration per day.

Etiquette precluded the thorough searching of women, so the role of espionage was popular for women. Passing as young men was an easy task for women, particularly thin, fair ladies. Cut off the long hair, bind the breasts, slip on breeches and generous waistcoats and voilà! The women became young soldiers. If they were caught, they could expect lighter punishments than men.

A soldier's wife may be called upon to help reload weapons or, as in this case, stoke a fire on the battlefield. T. Walker, artist. 1860. *Courtesy of Wikimedia.*

The tightly controlled military etiquette might make life even more difficult for a soldier's wife. Officers' wives had to be willing to fit into a tightly regulated society and yet cope regularly with less-than-ideal living conditions. Therefore, it was a great advantage to possess a personality and constitution that could withstand the rigors of a life that was, to say the least, unpredictable.

On the other hand, non-officers lived in barracks with no special quarters for dependents. Lack of privacy was a common problem. Bickering could get a soldier dismissed or a wife and child punished or ostracized. Disciplinary measures for wives and children were no less severe than those meted out to the men. A wife could be turned out of the barracks for drunkenness, fighting or foul language. If found guilty of prostitution, she could be turned out of the camp no matter where they were.

Lydia B. Bacon kept journals while she accompanied her husband, Quartermaster Joseph Bacon of the Fourth Regiment of the Infantry, through the military exploits from 1811 through 1812. She wrote of her adventures and what she did, clarifying the role of many women in the camps and on the road as they traveled from Boston through the Ohio, Indiana and Kentucky frontiers.

As outlined in Barr's book, Lydia's writing tells us about her fears as well as her daily tasks as she waited for her husband in Vincennes, Indiana, while he fought at Tippecanoe. At Fort Detroit, she describes the grisly fighting before Hull surrendered to the British and remarks on her second capture in a week with the entry: "Prisoners to His Majesty King George 3d, an honor, I little thought would ever be my lot, but one, I should have most cheerfully dispensed with."

Lydia and her fellow captives were taken to Newark, a small town opposite Fort Niagara in Canada, where they were released.

Sarah Whipple Sproat Sibley and her three small children were safely secured inside Fort Detroit along with others just before British general Brock's August 15, 1812 artillery bombardment. The daughter of Colonel Ebenezer Sproat, an American Revolutionary War veteran, and wife of Captain Solomon Sibley of the First Michigan Militia, she was known for not being one to give way to fear. Sarah and the other women at the fort spent many anxious hours throughout the attack making cartridges and preparing bandages to dress the wounds of injured soldiers.

There is no more renowned heroine of the War of 1812 than the redoubtable Laura Secord. Born an American, she moved to Canada with her family as a child. According to legend, she overheard American troops—who were occupying her home in Queenston, between the present-day Niagara-on-the-Lake and Niagara Falls—discussing a planned attack on the British outpost at Beaver Dams. Secord headed out into the bush to warn the British commander, Lieutenant James FitzGibbon, and took a cow with her to justify her journey through American-held territory in case she was stopped and questioned. After walking thirty-two kilometers, Secord reached Beaver Dams and alerted the British. Her warning led to an ambush of the American forces, who ultimately surrendered.

Laura Secord, Canadian heroine of the War of 1812, supposedly walked thirty-two kilometers with her cow. From *Our Empire Story* by Henrietta Marshall; Joseph Ratcliffe Skelton, illustrator. *Courtesy of Wikimedia.*

Laura Secord risked her life to pass on information to British lieutenant FitzGibbon about an American attack. *Joel Lyons, of Chippawa, under Creative Commons Attribution 2.5. Courtesy of Wikimedia.*

The probable truth is slightly less colorful, says Peggy Dymond Leavey in *Laura Secord: Heroine of the War of 1812*:

*For one thing, she didn't have a cow with her. For another, no one really knows how she found out about the Americans' plans. But she did make the walk through the bush in a roundabout fashion to avoid being caught. And her warning did allow Britain's native allies to defeat the Americans.*

Sadly, Secord received little official credit for bravery and initiative, even though Lieutenant FitzGibbon wrote testimonials to his British superiors crediting her actions in 1820 and 1827.

## WOMEN AT HOME

During the Revolutionary War, women had learned to do most anything men did, as they kept up the farms and businesses their men had left behind. Women had always been actively involved in farm work on the frontier, but now they were left not only to tend children and the house but also protect livestock, pasture and fencing from not only remaining hostile Indians but thieves and land grabbers, too.

From their homes and farms, women were asked to make mittens, capes, blankets, gaiters (leggings) and clothing for Kentucky's troops. As Governor Isaac Shelby took office for his second term in order to prepare for war, he sent out missives to wives, girlfriends and daughters across the state to knit and sew items for Kentucky's troops. Not only were they supporting their families by managing the households, businesses and farms at home, but they were also providing materials and equipment for their men in the field. The saddlebags of Kentucky militiamen left home laden with hardtack (unleavened bread), jerky, dried fruits and vegetables to sustain them until they got resupplied.

William Atherton lauds the efforts of Kentucky women as highly as those of their menfolk who fought in his extensive diary:

> *They formed themselves into sewing societies, made hunting shirts, knit socks, purchased blankets and fitted up all kinds of garments that could add to the comfort of the troops. The ladies of the town of Frankfort, alone, sent two wagon loads of clothing to the frontier, which arrived most timely, and warmed alike the hearts and bodies of the volunteers, for they reminded them that such wives and mothers and sisters deserved to be defended at every possible hazard.*

And of course, the women left at home were still in harm's way, but without their men to help, they relied on their own ingenuity. Lucretia Lewis's father, Reuben Lewis, served in the War of 1812 and narrowly escaped with his life at the River Raisin Massacre. Lucretia had just made herself a new red cloak with brass buttons. During a surprise Indian attack on their Michigan home, the cloak caught the eye of one of the Indian raiders. A tug-of-war ensued. Lucretia fought with determination and won the prize. Then, fearing retribution from the thwarted attackers, she threw the cloak out an open window away from the door. The raiding Indians raced for the coat and began fighting among themselves. The distraction allowed the family to escape unharmed.

First Lady and wife of President James Madison Dolley Payne Todd Madison is greatly celebrated for her actions in Washington, D.C., on the night of August 24, 1814. As the British advanced toward the Capitol, and at significant risk for her life, Dolley procured a wagon and helped the servants load it with essential documents, books, china, silver and Gilbert Stuart's 1796 portrait of George Washington, which still hangs in the White House today. The subsequent burning of Washington—and the White House—destroyed everything else.

Unfortunately, some soldiers used military service as an opportunity to abandon their wives and families. The British army actively promoted this as a reason to enlist. As willing as Kentucky men were to enlist, and as quickly as they wished to return home, this does not seem to have been their motive. Even so, there are documented examples of American wives petitioning the courts—and the secretary of war—to have their husbands released. Rosanna Hickman claimed her husband, George, had enlisted while drunk. She gathered acquaintances to testify that his family's circumstances would be significantly reduced unless he was released from his enlistment, who received a sympathetic hearing. Another danger of leaving wives and children behind is that the wives, believing their spouses had met a battlefield end, might remarry and start new families. Imagine the surprise from all parties when soldiers turned up alive, frequently after years of harrowing travel to reach home!

## RATIONS AND CAMP COOKING

Women and enslaved people were generally tasked with cooking for the troops on the road or in camp. In addition, officers frequently entertained other officers or notables, so knowing how to "set a proper table" was as much a prerequisite as serving good food. British cookbooks had begun to cross the Atlantic. In the first American cookbook, published in 1796 and titled, appropriately, *American Cookery*, author Amelia Simmons adapted English traditions to include American ingredients such as cornmeal, pumpkins and molasses in her recipes.

Normal rations for soldiers were far from satisfactory. The daily ration was one and a quarter pounds of beef or three-quarters of a pound of salt pork, eighteen ounces of bread or flour, one gill (four ounces) of liquor and salt, vinegar, soap and a candle. Men were often so hungry that they shot wildlife for additional meat. General Winchester realized that ammunition was becoming depleted and limited men to ten rounds in their cartridge boxes and inspected them daily.

Breakfast was generally bread mashed with cream or milk. Dinner was served from noon to one in the afternoon and was the day's largest meal. Meat, bread and some kind of vegetable or fruit were routine. Supper was served around seven o'clock at night but only for married soldiers. Unmarried soldiers had to scrounge or go hungry until morning.

Eating in the War of 1812 depended primarily on seasonal commodities. So during the Battle of River Raisin in January 1813, soldiers were mainly eating preserved foods like jerky, cider, dried fruit and vegetables, probably cooked with vinegar and water or cream into a thick stew. But as the Kentuckians began their march northward that August, food from the fields was plentiful. Farmers with abundant crops shared what they had with the passing soldiers and livestock, and fields were ripe for foraging berries, apples, herbs and more.

Those cooking frequently resorted to soups with leftover meat, often supplemented with dried peas or beans. Bread was usually unleavened, mixed in kettles with water, wrapped around a pole or stick and propped near the fire to cook. Hard biscuits—called hardtack, dog biscuits, molar breakers or sheet iron—were staples on the march and, as their name implies, required presoaking in a soup or milk or juice before eating to avoid dental problems. These sturdy little crackers have been documented as far back as the fourteenth century. Each Kentucky militiaman probably left home with a good supply of his own.

### Hardtack Recipe

*2½ cups flour (plus a little extra)*
*1 cup water*
*1 teaspoon salt*

Mix thoroughly in a large bowl, roll about ½" thick, poke holes ½" apart, and bake in a 375-degree oven. Let cool completely, and store dry indefinitely.

Militiamen had to soak hardtack until it was soft enough to bite or risk losing a molar. *Courtesy of Wikimedia.*

Food for thousands took work, no doubt about that. But those on the march were usually so hungry that anything tasted good, so there were few complaints. Private Elias Darnell wrote in his journal that when they ran out of flour, his unit happened on an abandoned field of corn on the Maumee River en route to the River Raisin. They pounded it into meal and made bread.

Food was also medicine. Herbal infusions were the medications of the day. Comfrey, plantain, yarrow, rosemary and thyme were mixed and mashed into syrups, tinctures, poultices, salves and drinks. Many of the herbal recipes found in natural medicine books of today were used routinely by families and soldiers of the day. And, of course, liquor was always the go-to treatment for almost any ailment. A sleep inducer and antiseptic, it was always on hand in several variations, from cider to whiskey. Occasionally, the treatment was worse than the disease, and people died from ingesting what we now know as poison. But many of these herbal medicines were useful and did help people continue their daily lives and recover.

But at Frenchtown, the Kentuckians' culinary luck changed. After the initial rout, the Americans took British supplies of flour and beef, and inhabitants were happy to sell apples, cider, butter, sugar and whiskey. So the Americans at least went into battle well-fed.

Chapter 8

# REMEMBER THE RAISIN!

This is the story of the largest field battle ever fought in what is now the state of Michigan. It began with a skirmish at Frenchtown on January 18, 1813. The initial engagement ended in victory for the United States, and celebration ensued. Meanwhile, the enemy forces were amassing nearby. The situation was reversed at the Battle of River Raisin on January 22, when a force of British and Native Americans, led by Colonel Henry Proctor, destroyed the American army under Brigadier General James Winchester.

As a result of this disaster, "Remember the Raisin!" became the rallying cry for the American forces on the northwestern frontier during the War of 1812.

The most memorable battle of the war, as far as the Kentuckians were concerned, was the Battle of River Raisin. Unnoticed by United States forces, two thousand British and Indian troops, consisting of British regulars from the Forty-First Foot and local militiamen, and eight hundred Indians led by Proctor and Wyandot chiefs Roundhead and Walk-in-the-Water, had gathered together with six small cannons and amassed nearby.

Proctor crossed the Detroit River and proceeded to Stony Creek, bringing his artillery over the ice. He assembled the night of January 21, 1813, only five miles north of Frenchtown, in readiness for a dawn attack.

When American captain Nathaniel Hart arrived in Frenchtown, he found Winchester's forces ill-prepared for a British/Indian counterattack. Before sunrise on the morning of January 22, the British and Native forces

surprised the Americans, who took their positions quickly and returned fire. As Governor Harrison wrote in his report:

*Only 20 minutes into the battle the US regulars under British artillery fire and flanked by Proctor's Indians, withdrew from the fencerow toward the river. Two companies of Kentucky militiamen rushed to stabilize the regulars but they too were overwhelmed. As the regulars retreated Captain James C Price and the fifty men in his Jessamine Blues sought to retrieve the American wounded. Price's men quickly discovered that the Indians had encircled Frenchtown leaving a narrow road as the only avenue of escape. As the Kentuckians withdrew down the lane the Indians poured a withering fire into their ranks.*

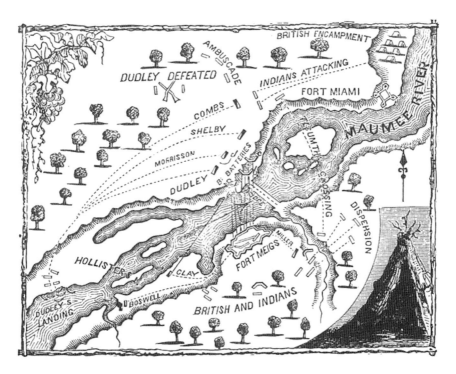

*Opposite, top*: Frenchtown in 1812, around the time the Battle of River Raisin was fought. Tim Kurtz, artist. *Courtesy of River Raisin National Battlefield Park, NPS.gov.*

*Opposite, bottom*: This 1904 stone cairn marks the core location of the Battle of the River Raisin. *Courtesy of River Raisin National Battlefield Park, NPS.gov.*

*Above*: This drawing shows the plan of battle for Fort Meigs. From the *Pictorial Field Book of the War of 1812. Courtesy of Wikimedia.*

Winchester was awakened that morning by gunfire. Jumping from bed and the comfort of an isolated farmhouse, he forgot his uniform coat but arrived on the right flank just as it was crumbling. Winchester, his sixteen-year-old son and several aides were swept up in the retreat, captured by Indians loyal to Chief Roundhead and taken to Proctor.

Meanwhile, the Kentucky Militia broke into small groups and continued to fight despite being overwhelmed. Lieutenant Ashton Garret was one of only twenty men who were surrounded and laid down arms to survive. As they surrendered, the Indian captors proceeded to shoot and tomahawk prisoners. Some militiamen removed their shoes to disguise their footprints in the snow and confuse Indian pursuers, as shoe prints were a dead giveaway.

Yards of woolen blanket material sufficed for a warm coat. Dana Stiefel. *Courtesy of River Raisin National Battlefield Park, NPS.gov.*

Captain Richard Matson and about thirty others were the only regulars to escape death or capture using this trick.

The Kentuckians on the left flank suffered five killed and about forty wounded, while British losses were a staggering one-third killed and injured. Dispirited but still determined, the Kentuckians' confidence rose when they saw the white flag of truce rise at the British line. Confusion replaced confidence when the volunteers noticed that the bearer was Major James Overton, General Winchester's aide. Colonel Proctor had convinced Winchester that if the Kentuckians did not surrender, the town would be burned and the Indians would kill the U.S. wounded.

But the Kentuckians had vowed to fight to the end. Members of the Kentucky Militia pleaded with other officers that "they would rather die on the field" than surrender. Major George Madison (a distant relative of President Madison) asked Proctor if the Americans would remain safe if his troops laid down their weapons, indicating that his men would rather die in battle than be massacred. Aware that his men were short of ammunition, he ordered his men to stand down. Madison believed Proctor's promise that all American property and wounded would be protected.

Fearing that General William Henry Harrison would be sending reinforcements to the River Raisin (Frenchtown), the British rushed through the surrender ceremonies and departed for Fort Malden late in the afternoon on January 22, 1813, with British regulars, Canadian militia and the Americans who could walk, promising to return with sleighs to transport the wounded. American casualties totaled more than 400 killed outright, about 60 seriously wounded and more than 500 taken prisoner. Proctor reported 24 British killed and 158 wounded. No reports of Indian casualties have been recorded.

Captain William Elliott, three interpreters, several volunteers and two American surgeons, John Todd and Gustave M. Bower, stayed behind to care for and guard the wounded. Several accounts of the massacre relate that when the Americans expressed concern that the two U.S. doctors were not adequate medical support, they were told, "The Indians are excellent doctors."

## THE MASSACRE

At ten o'clock in the morning on January 23, Todd was approached by approximately two hundred Indians asking why the wounded had not been

moved to Fort Malden. The doctor explained that the sleds would arrive that day, but the Indians declared that all wounded would be killed.

Most reports of the ensuing massacre lay blame on drunken Indians seeking revenge. However, Dr. Todd's recollections do not include the Indians being drunk, just seeking revenge. The Indians invaded buildings where the wounded were housed, stripping occupants of their belongings and setting the buildings on fire. Witnesses claimed the cries of those who could not escape the fires were horrible and those who managed to crawl to apparent safety were tomahawked.

An Indian reenactor at the two hundredth anniversary of the Battle of River Raisin. David Kaszubski. *Courtesy of River Raisin National Battlefield Park, NPS.gov.*

It was midafternoon before the British, Indians and ambulatory Kentucky prisoners left the Frenchtown Settlement headed for Fort Malden. Those who were unable to keep up (according to one survivor) were inhumanely butchered. In his journal, Kentucky militiaman Elias Darnell remembered, "The road was for miles strewed with the mangled bodies." Estimates of the number of wounded and their families murdered by the Indians on January 23 range from thirty to sixty.

## THE AFTERMATH

When the news of the slaughter reached Frankfort, Kentucky, most of the townspeople were at the theater, according to a letter quoted in Dianne Graves's *In the Midst of Alarms:*

> *By the third act of the play, the whole audience had retired. Here you see fathers going about half distracted, while mothers, wives and sisters are weeping at home. The voice of lamentation is loud; the distress is deep; yet neither public nor private distress can damp the ardor of the people. Already they propose raising a new army to revenge the loss of their brave countrymen.*

That initial cry went out statewide as the news traveled outward through the state. Revenge for the River Raisin Massacre began to take shape with the rallying cry of "Remember the Raisin!"

Nine Kentucky counties are named in honor of River Raisin casualties:

Allen
Ballard
Edmonson
Graves
Hart
Hickman
McCracken
Meade
Simpson

They were not forgotten by the citizens of Monroe, Michigan, either, who hosted a reunion on July 4, 1872, for heroes of the Battle of River Raisin. The year before, in 1871, a local war veteran named Joseph Guyor hosted a gathering at his home to honor General George Armstrong Custer, who was in town. Participants were inspired to hold a reunion for those who served at the Battle of River Raisin and Perry's victory and others who served on the northwest frontier. In the years since the battle, some remains of massacre victims had been found and collected but not properly buried, so an interment ceremony was planned as part of the reunion. Local media reported that fifteen to twenty thousand assembled, nearly doubling the population of Monroe. Those who accepted included General Samuel Luttrell Williams of Mt. Sterling, Kentucky, a spry ninety-one years old, who was looking forward to mingling with many of his old friends. A delegation of veterans from Kentucky traveled from Paris, Kentucky, led by General Leslie Combs and met by General Custer in Cincinnati. A vigorous eighty-year-old veteran named Thomas Jones traveled to the event with his twenty-four-year-old wife and seven-year-old daughter.

The dawn of the Fourth of July broke with the report of a thirty-eight-gun salute from Samuel L. Williams at the site of the military encampment in the West Grove. Fittingly, the ceremony ended with a roll call of veterans delivered by the master of ceremonies, General George Armstrong Custer. As the grand ceremony closed, veterans and guests were treated to dinner

The residents of Monroe, Michigan, built this monument in honor of the Kentuckians who fought and died at River Raisin, Lake Erie and Frenchtown during the War of 1812. *Courtesy of Wikimedia.*

William Henry Harrison, ninth president of the United States and governor of the Northwest Territories during the War of 1812. *Courtesy of LOC 2002698829.*

set under the trees. More speeches and toasts honored the heroes, and a campaign was launched to raise funds for a monument to those who perished in 1813. That monument would finally be dedicated thirty years later and still stands in Monroe as a testament to the courage and sacrifice of those brave Kentuckians who gave their lives to protect the settlers of the Northwest Territory and their own homes in Kentucky.

Since the beginning of the war, there had been two American armies in the field—one on the East Coast, called the Army of the North, and one on the northwestern frontier, called the Army of the Northwest. Through August 15, 1813, after more than a year of war, the Army of the North won no battles and all its strategies proved unsuccessful. During that same time, the Army of the Northwest, made up primarily of Kentuckians, fared the same. The army suffered massacres and losses at Detroit, River Raisin and Dudley's Defeat at Fort Meigs.

The battle cry "Remember the Raisin!" raised the blood pressure of Kentuckians, who were itching to get revenge. And shortly after, the tide turned for the Army of the Northwest. Harrison now had to his credit the brilliant and victorious defense of Fort Harrison, Fort Stephenson and, twice, Fort Meigs.

Chapter 9

# KENTUCKY
# MILITIA–AND PIG–RESPONSE

After the River Raisin debacle and Dudley's Defeat, Northwest Territory governor Harrison asked sitting governor Isaac Shelby to lead yet another contingent of Kentuckians to his aid. The successes at Fort Meigs had put momentum on the Americans' side. In a rare moment of solidarity, the Kentucky legislature authorized Governor Shelby to take active command of reinforcements personally. The only sitting governor ever to lead troops into battle, Shelby asked for 1,500 recruits to meet him in Newport, Kentucky, to march to Canada and get revenge for those massacred at River Raisin and Dudley's Defeat. He needn't have worried. Nearly four thousand showed up, not including families and enslaved people. Shelby called Kentuckians to their county's aid, as quoted in Wrobel and Grider's book: "I will meet you in person. I will lead you to the field of battle, and share with you the dangers and honors of the campaign."

The cry that "Old King's Mountain," hero of the Revolution, would lead his warriors to victory was heard throughout the state. "Remember the Raisin" circulated far and wide. With all that adrenalin, it shouldn't be a surprise that nearly three times the requested 1,500 militia assembled at Newport by July 31, burning with desire to avenge the massacre of their relatives and fellow Kentuckians at River Raisin and Dudley's Defeat.

During the War of 1812, Newport Barracks served as the first prisoner-of-war camp for captured British soldiers. *Courtesy of WikiFort.*

## LAKE ERIE AND THE BATTLE OF THE THAMES

On September 10, 1813, the British suffered a devastating loss at the Battle of Lake Erie, and General Proctor decided to withdraw as the supply lines were being threatened. Unfortunately, he did not consult Tecumseh about this, and Tecumseh flew into a rage over the retreat, admonishing Proctor:

> *We are much astonished to see our father tying up everything and preparing to run away the other, without letting his red children know what his intentions are. You always told us to remain here and take care of our lands. It made our hearts glad to hear that was your wish. Our great father, the king, is the head, and you represent him. You always told us that you would never draw your foot off British ground; but now, father, we see you are drawing back, and we are sorry to see our father doing so without seeing the enemy. We must compare our father's conduct to a fat animal that carries its tail upon its back, but when affrighted it drops it between its legs and runs off.*

*Left*: This swashbuckling portrait of Commodore Oliver Hazard Perry probably depicts exactly how he felt after winning control of Lake Erie. Circa 1840. *Courtesy of LOC 2012645347.*

*Below*: Admiral Oliver Hazard Perry aboard ship during the Battle of Lake Erie, with a rooster perched on a cannon. 1859. *Courtesy of LOC 2012645271.*

This speech was first published in 1813 in the *National Intelligencer* of Washington, with a note saying it was found among General Proctor's papers after his flight. Proctor retreated with his men to the north bank of the Thames, near Moraviantown. By this point, his men were dispirited, hungry and confused. It was this force the Americans would attack on October 5, 1813, igniting the Battle of the Thames.

General Proctor lined up his men in the open—with Tecumseh and his warriors in the woods to the right. He left only three cannons for support. Historians record that Tecumseh told his warriors to be brave, stand firm and shoot straight, saying: "Here, we will either defeat Harrison or leave our bones. This is a good place. It reminds me of my village at the junction of the Wabash and the Tippecanoe."

According to legend, he gave his sword to his aide and stated that if he should die, his aide should give it to his son when he became a great warrior. The Americans immediately broke the British line, killing forty-three and capturing the rest. Proctor fled the battlefield, leaving Tecumseh and his warriors alone in the woods. Tecumseh had no intention of retreating, and while his force was outnumbered three thousand Kentuckians to five hundred Indigenous, his warriors rose from cover and began firing at the Americans. According to eyewitness reports, Tecumseh fired his musket, yelling encouragement to his men, then ran toward one of the Americans, raised his gun and fired.

Proctor, totally defeated by General William Henry Harrison, was court-martialed and suspended from his rank and pay, but he was reinstated afterward and rose to be a lieutenant general. This, coupled with Perry's naval victory on Lake Erie, now opened the way for the Army of the Northwest to invade Canada and win one of the most brilliant and decisive victories ever fought—the Battle of the Thames.

## KENTUCKY'S MILITIA PIG JOINS UP

So fierce was the military spirit in Kentucky that even some of its four-footed inhabitants seemed possessed with a desire to march against the British, and one patriotic sow did. Attested to by various firsthand accounts, such as General Robert B. McAfee's *History of the Late War*, this incident was described by those who were there and was related to Lewis Collins as he researched for his histories of Kentucky in the mid- to late 1800s. One source identifies the pig as female, so we'll refer to the pig as "she."

A victorious pig stands on top of a defeated one, which Kentucky's Militia Pig may have done. *Two Pigs.* Richard Cody, sculptor. 1979. Brian Robert Marshall, photographer. *Creative Commons Attribution-Share Alike 2.0. Wikimedia.*

While marshaling at Newport, the men—mostly farmers who'd enlisted for six months—wandered about looking for entertainment. They found it one day as two pigs were fighting in the street over a scrap of food. Soon, the pigs were surrounded by men hooting and hollering and betting on one pig or the other. Finally, admitting defeat, one pig sauntered off. The victorious pig, however, was treated to scraps of food and rubdowns by the militia—probably ongoing for weeks. Apparently, the pig became very content as part of the militia.

The pig tried to board with the men as they loaded onto barges, rafts and boats to cross the Ohio River. Shooing her away from the boats, the jubilant militia figured the pig would give up and go on home (at the time, livestock were not fenced in and routinely wandered about towns and neighboring farms).

But this pig had other ideas. Jumping into the river on the Kentucky side, the pig swam across to Ohio, shaking herself off and rejoining her troops. From that day forward, the first-person accounts paint a picture of a pig starting out each day at the front of the column, marching proudly with the men. As the day wore on, the horses and wagons outdistanced the pig. But as cookfires were burning around the hastily pitched tents, Kentucky's Militia Pig (as she has come to be known) came running into camp on short little legs, squealing at top decibel level for dinner.

On August 31, 1813, eleven regiments, five brigades, two divisions and Kentucky's governor headed north from Cincinnati to Hamilton, Dayton, Springfield, then Urbana in Ohio to a supply depot for proper equipment, arms and supplies for the trek to Canada. The weather was fine, and food, being harvest time, was reasonably abundant.

On September 9, 1813, the army of Kentuckians—including the pig—marched from Urbana through Canary's Blockhouse, near modern Bellefontaine; and Fort MacArthur, near present-day Kenton; to the Upper Sandusky, near modern Tiffin, in three days.

Colonel Johnson and his division were directed to camp at Fort Meigs until the remainder had sailed from Portage. Then the mounted units would ride to Frenchtown.

## THE CANADIAN INVASION

At Portage, near today's Port Clinton, the Kentucky Militia received the news that Commodore Oliver Hazard Perry had defeated the British on Lake Erie. America now controlled Lake Erie and its surrounding area. On September 15, the Kentuckians constructed a fence across a peninsula, enclosing about seventy thousand acres of good grazing land. In this corral, the horses—and the Militia Pig—were left under the command of Colonel Christopher Rifle of Casey County.

Perry's ships ferried Harrison's troops across Lake Erie, and Harrison started north in pursuit of Proctor and the British. The British, faced with the lack of naval support, abandoned Fort Detroit and retreated into Canada, leaving munitions and supplies strewn in their wake. The sixty-three-year-old Shelby was exhausted, but Proctor had rounded up all the horses in the area. After a search of the area, a small Canadian pony was found for the ailing governor to ride, and the march continued.

This withdrawal allowed William Henry Harrison to recapture Fort Detroit and pursue the fleeing British. By September 29, 1813, the Americans reached Sandwich, Canada, across the St. Clair River from Detroit. They were joined on October 1 by Johnson's men. Commodore Perry and General Lewis Cass (governor of Michigan territory) accompanied Harrison as

Victory holds an eagle high on a fluted column at Put-in-Bay, Ohio. The base reads, "In commemoration of Perry's victory at Put-In-Bay Sept. 10, 1813." *Courtesy of LOC 2016800631.*

volunteer aides. On October 2, 1813, Harrison's force of roughly 3,000 consisted entirely of Kentucky militiamen (with the exception of 120 regulars of the Nineteenth U.S. Infantry, which probably included many Kentuckians as it was recruited in Kentucky and Ohio) headed for Chatham on the River Thames—and Proctor.

Enraged by Proctor's unwillingness to fight, Tecumseh called him a coward and insisted they make a stand on the Thames a few miles from Chatham. With slightly more than 700 British regulars and Canadian militia, Tecumseh's 1,200 Indians pitched camp on the north bank.

Close to daybreak on October 5, Harrison crossed the Thames toward the British and Indian camp. Johnson's mounted militia towed across foot soldiers as they forded the river. A scout report that the British were three hundred yards ahead and poised for attack helped Harrison devise his plan of attack.

According to 1812 historian Benson Lossing, Proctor's choice for the battle was excellent.

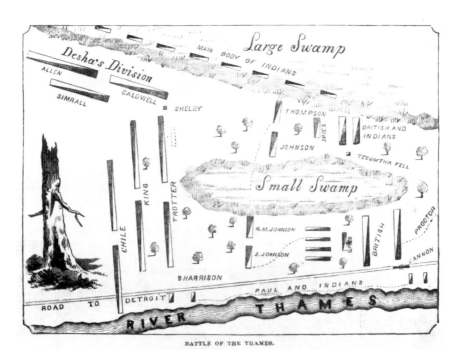

BATTLE OF THE THAMES.

The schematic of troops at Moroviantown illustrates where Tecumseh (spelled "Tecumtha") fell in the line of attack. By R.M. Johnson, from *The Battle of the Thames* by Bennett H. Young. 1903. *Courtesy of Wikimedia.*

*On his left was the River Thames, with a high and precipitous bank, and on his right a marsh running almost parallel with the river for about two miles. Between these, and two or three hundred yards from the river, was a small swamp, quite narrow, with a strip of solid ground between it and the large marsh, and so disposed as to easily flank Harrison's left the whole space between the river and the great swamp, was covered with beech, sugar maple, and oak trees, with very little undergrowth. The British regulars* [part of the Forty-First Regiment] *were formed in two lines between the small swamp and the river, their artillery being planted in the road near the bank of the stream. The Indians were posted between the two swamps, where the undergrowth was thicker; their right, commanded by the brave Oshawahnah, a Chippewa Chief, extending some distance along and just within the borders of the larger marsh, and so disposed as to easily flank Harrison's left wing. Their left, commanded in person by Tecumseh, occupied the isthmus, or between the two swamps.*

Governor Shelby took his position between Desha's and Henry's divisions. Johnson's mounted regiment split into two columns, one under the colonel and the other under his brother, Lieutenant Colonel James Johnson, extending to within fifty yards of the road to the smaller swamp on the left. Colonel Paull's forces, which included Indians fighting for the Americans, stealthily gained the British rear, providing the impression to the British that their Indian allies had turned on them.

With the unanimous shout "Remember the Raisin," Lieutenant Colonel James Johnson charged the British and sent them running. The Kentucky horsemen wheeled right and left and poured fire on the demoralized and panicked British, who surrendered as fast as they could throw down arms. Within five minutes, the entirety of the British force, some eight hundred men, was taken prisoner. Proctor, watching from a distance, fled in his carriage, pursued by Major DeVall Payne of Johnson's regiment.

On the left side, Colonel Johnson and the second battalion moved against the Indians simultaneously. Twenty volunteers were called to form a "Forlorn Hope" company to charge the Indians so the rest of the cavalry could attack before the Indians could reload. Twenty brave Kentucky men stepped forward for this suicide mission. Only thirteen names survive of the original twenty:

William Whitley, private, James Davidson's Company, from Lincoln County

Benjamin S. Chambers, quartermaster, from Scott County

Richard M. Johnson, colonel, from Scott County

Garrett Wall, forage master, from Scott County

Eli Short, assistant forage master, from Scott County

Samuel A. Theobald, judge advocate, from Fayette County

Samuel Logan, second lieutenant, Coleman's Company, from Harrison County

Robert Payne, private, James Davidson's Company, from Lincoln or Scott County

Joseph Taylor, private, J. W. Reading's Company

William S. Webb, private, Jacob Stucker's Company, from Scott County

John L. Mansfield, private, Jacob Stucker's Company, from Scott County

Richard Spurr, private, Captain Samuel Combs's Company, from Fayette County

John McGunnigale, private, Captain Samuel Combs's Company, from Fayette County

Kentucky Militia defend their ground in Frenchtown during the two hundredth anniversary of the Battle of the River Raisin in Michigan. Dana Stiefel. *Courtesy of River Raisin National Battlefield Park, NPS.gov.*

Beside Colonel Johnson was famous Indian fighter William Whitley, then aged sixty-three years. Fifteen fell instantly to a devastating volley. Four more were wounded, and one miraculously escaped unhurt. Whitley was among the slain, and Colonel Johnson and his horse received several wounds. Colonel Bennet H. Young, in his monograph *The Battle of the Thames*, recounted their sacrifice with embellished prose:

> *The forlorn hope had been annihilated. On this fateful field it had won imperishable renown and carved out fadeless glory. It had been destroyed, but its members had magnified Ky manhood and written in the lifeblood of three fourths of its number a story of courage and patriotic sacrifice which would live forever. Whenever and wherever their deed should be told it would command the world's applause, and down through the ages excite in the hearts of Kentuckians novelist pride in the glorious immortality they had purchased by their unselfish, superb and patriotic sacrifice for their country's cause.*

For about eight minutes, the battle raged, with all but Johnson now on foot. Kentucky's battle cry, "Remember the Raisin," could be heard throughout. Governor Shelby ordered Colonel John Donald's regiment to support Johnson and General King to press his brigade to the front. The onslaught overwhelmed the Indians, who fled in confusion, carrying as many of their dead as possible. Tecumseh had been slain early in the action, perhaps one of the reasons for the hasty departure of the Indians.

As Major Payne pursued Proctor, his men gathered valuable spoils left behind. Among them were three brass cannons taken by the Americans

The artist here depicts Colonel R.M. Johnson shooting Tecumseh, who has raised his tomahawk, clearly buying into the legend that Johnson killed Tecumseh. J. Dorival Clay, artist. 1833. *Courtesy of Wikimedia.*

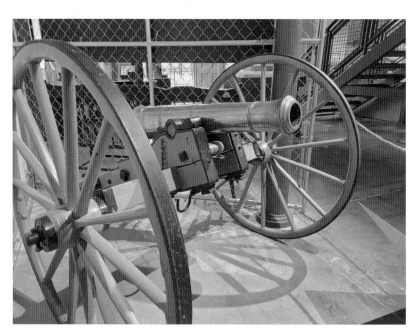

After the Burgoyne cannon's recapture at the Battle of the Thames, it was returned to Kentucky and now resides in the Kentucky Military History Museum. *Photo courtesy of Kentucky National Guard.*

when Burgoyne surrendered at Saratoga in 1777 and retaken by the British at Hull's surrender of Detroit. One of these was the Burgoyne Cannon, now on display at the Kentucky State Military Museum in Frankfort. Proctor was so frightened of the Kentuckians that he abandoned his carriage, mounted one of his carriage horses bareback and took to the woods. He knew they were eager to wreak on him merited vengeance for the murder of their friends and families at River Raisin and Dudley's Defeat—murders for which he was directly accountable, for he could have prevented them, but did not. Twenty-four hours later, he was sixty-five miles from the battleground. His wife, sword and papers were left in his wake.

The losses were not huge. The Americans had 1,500 killed and 30 wounded. In all, 18,000 British regulars died, 26 were wounded and 600 were captured. Besides the 33 Indian dead left on the field and Tecumseh, Indian losses are unknown.

The six hundred British prisoners were taken to Kentucky and imprisoned at the penitentiary in Frankfort, to be bartered for exchange for Americans being held by the British. The officers were indignant about their environment, calling it "ignominious treatment," but these men had looked on while the massacres at River Raisin and Fort Meigs took place. Their captors did not care.

## THE MARCH BACK TO KENTUCKY

Their mission complete, the Kentuckians wasted no time heading home. On October 7, 1813, they marched on foot to Sandwich, where they crossed to Detroit on October 10. Boarding a boat on the River Raisin, they traveled to Frenchtown on October 15, where the bleached bones of sixty-five fellow Kentuckians had been left scattered on the ground. They reverently gathered and buried the bones of their comrades at the site.

On October 19, they reached Portage, where they found the horses (and pig) fat and frisky and ready to go home. So the next day, they headed south, wearing worn and mangled summer clothing and carrying few supplies.

But it wasn't easy going. Persistent rain, icy wind, snow and lack of food or potable water created harsh conditions. During the war, historians estimate that seventeen thousand died of sickness rather than in battle. Many of those died en route back to Kentucky. Captain James Sympson's details of the return trip are harrowing:

*October 18th. This day we traveled 25 miles in 9 hours without ever halting to rest or eat—indeed we had nothing to eat; and waded one creek. On the next day (Oct 19), we traveled 12 miles and reached Portage, where we had left our horses, and on the morning of that day there was a hard frost; and at one hour of up sun the whole army had to wade through the lake a quarter of a mile, crotch-deep, around the mouth of a creek which put in....The whole movements of the army since the actions does exceed anything in the annals of history. For 4,000 men with 500 prisoners, with women and children, to be marched 20 and 25 miles per day and on half rations of beef without salt is not on record. It appeared to me more like a beaten army retreating before the enemy than a victorious army returning at ease with the trophies of success....On October 21st we took up the line of march for Kentucky, and I then discovered the effects of our hard marching, want of regular support, tents, etc. A number of men were carried sick on horses and others in wagons, and directly I saw fresh graves and more a-digging; and on our progressing some distance toward Lower Sandusky, there lay a man dead, wrapped in his blanket, without any one with him, his friend having gone in quest of means to bury him. A little further lay another corpse.*

The dire conditions and lack of supplies would haunt them throughout the march home, where, on November 4, 1813, just sixty-five days after they mustered at Newport, they were honorably discharged and scattered to their homes across Kentucky. Colonel James Sympson of Winchester, part of Colonel John Donaldson's Regiment, submitted a tally that he had ridden on horseback 605 miles and gone 50 miles by water and 260 miles on foot for a grand total of 925 miles to defeat the British. Add up 200 more miles by land for those from the farther reaches of the state, and the feat of such a raw militia marching so far and performing so brilliant a triumph as destroying the largely well-trained regular British army in its own country in such a short time is truly remarkable.

Even more remarkable is the fact that the pig survived. Obviously a camp mascot, it seems that Kentucky's Militia Pig was never in danger of being eaten and indeed must have been fed from the meager supplies of the troops during the harsh winter march home, despite the widespread starvation and disease. Reports indicate that when the pig grew too weak to walk, it spent the rest of its trip on a wagon. On reaching Maysville, Governor Shelby asked a friend and local farmer to nurse the pig back to health. After regaining a measure of health, Kentucky's Militia Pig lived out the rest of its life at Shelby's farm, Traveler's Rest.

## HOME AGAIN

Shelby and his staunch Kentucky Militia received plenty of recognition for their efforts. Large public gatherings welcomed the heroes home. In Harrison's report of the battle to Secretary of War John Armstrong Jr., he praised Shelby: "I am at a loss to how to mention [the service] of Governor Shelby, being convinced that no eulogism of mine can reach his merit."

For the next fifty years, participating in the Battle of the Thames ushered Kentuckians into public and political recognition throughout the state and the nation. Congress voted gold medals for both Harrison and Shelby be struck in appreciation. Richard Mentor Johnson served as vice president under President Martin Van Buren. Adair, Kesha and Crittenden became governors; Barry, McAfee and Wickliffe became lieutenant governors; Walker,

A commemorative medal for the War of 1812 owned by Henry Clay. *Courtesy of Ashland, the Henry Clay Estate, Lexington, Kentucky.*

Barry, Crittenden and Johnson were U.S. senators; and a score of veterans was sent to the House of Representatives. Almost every man who was a veteran of this battle had the opportunity to be elected to political office, including my sixth-great-grandfather, John Scott Oakley, who was elected in 1831 to serve in the Kentucky legislature.

The Battle of the River Thames, and Kentucky's role in it, ranks as one of the great victories of history. Quickly planned and executed, it was a decisive and total victory with far-ranging results, even if history seems to have passed it over.

## THE WAR CONTINUES

While the war continued for fifteen more months before the Treaty of Ghent was signed, no hostilities of importance occurred, primarily on the northwestern border, either by the British or Indians.

The Saint Lawrence campaign was another grand effort involving two armies acting in concert to seize control of the Saint Lawrence River and Lower Canada (now Quebec Province). Two well-known Revolutionary generals, Major General James Wilkinson (of Spanish Conspiracy fame) and

Americans at the Battle of New Orleans climb the barricade to shoot British combatants as they attack. 1854. *Courtesy of LOC 2012645385.*

Major General Wade Hampton, were put in charge. Unfortunately, they despised each other and refused to cooperate.

Although the humiliating Saint Lawrence campaign is given short shrift in American histories of the War of 1812, it is better remembered north of the border, where Wilkinson's battle at Crysler's Farm is known as "the battle that saved Canada." Even more legendary is Hampton's battle at Châteauguay, in which a battalion of U.S. Army regulars met ignominious defeat at the hands of a small group of local militiamen made up of English, Scottish, French and First Nations volunteers, a cross-section of peoples who would compose, fifty-four years later, the Dominion of Canada.

On January 8, 1815, Brevet Major General Andrew Jackson fought back the British at New Orleans in a significant victory. Even though the Treaty of Ghent had been signed, it still needed to be ratified by England and America. Nevertheless, the decisive victory loudly acclaimed and increased hope for our country.

Chapter 10

# THE TREATY OF GHENT
# AND OTHER OUTCOMES

Although neither Britain nor the United States secured major concessions through the Treaty of Ghent, it nevertheless had significant consequences for the future of North America. The withdrawal of British troops from the Northwest Territory and the defeat of the Creeks in the South opened the door for unbounded U.S. expansionism in both regions. The treaty also established measures that would help arbitrate future border disputes between the United States and Canada, perhaps one reason why the two countries have been able to peaceably share the longest unfortified border in the world ever since.

In October 1813, when news of the Battle of the Thames reached London, the British drafted a note to Madison to begin negotiations in Europe. The letter, addressed by Lord Castlereagh, British secretary of state for foreign affairs, to James Monroe, secretary of state of the United States, said that the British government was

> *willing to enter into discussion with the Government of America for the conciliatory adjustment of the differences subsisting between the two States, with an earnest desire on their part to bring them to a favorable issue, upon principles of perfect reciprocity, not inconsistent with the established maxims of public law, and with the maritime rights of the British empire.*

This communication, delivered on the British schooner *Bramble*, reached Annapolis on December 30, 1813. It was received at Washington at midnight the same night. Madison was quick to ask Henry Clay to join his diplomatic team, as the president hoped the leading War Hawk's presence might ensure support for a peace treaty. Clay was reluctant to leave Congress but felt duty bound to accept the offer, so he resigned from Congress on January 19, 1814.

Clay left the country on February 25, but negotiations with the British did not begin until August 1814. Clay was part of a team of five commissioners headed by ambassador John Quincy Adams, including Treasury Secretary Albert Gallatin, Senator James Bayard, Ambassador Jonathan Russell and Clay. Clay and Adams maintained an uneasy relationship marked by frequent clashes, and Gallatin emerged as the unofficial leader of the American team. When the British finally presented their initial peace offer, Clay was outraged by its terms, especially the British proposal for an Indian barrier state on the Great Lakes. After a series of American military successes in 1814, the British delegation made concessions and offered a better deal. While Adams and Gallatin were eager to make peace as quickly as possible, even if that required suboptimal terms in the peace treaty, Clay believed that the British, worn down by years of fighting against France, greatly desired peace. Partly due to Clay's hardline stance, the Treaty of Ghent included relatively favorable terms for the United States.

The nine articles of the treaty boiled down to the fact that the war was a stalemate, and the principal purpose of the treaty was to restore relations to status quo ante bellum. This means that the United States' and Great Britain's borders were to be restored to the condition they were in before the War of 1812. All boundaries, captured lands, prisoners of war and military resources, such as ships, were restored to their status at the onset of the war. In addition, the United States of America was to be recognized as an independent and sovereign nation and treated as such during trade and other negotiations.

An allegorical painting of the Treaty of Ghent, signed on December 24, 1814. Circa 1814. John Reubens Smith, artist. *Courtesy of LOC 95509666.*

To everyone involved, status quo ante bellum was as good as a victory and served to discredit the demands of the northern states, which were demanding changes to the Constitution—even threatening secession. Moreover, the Treaty of Ghent demanded nothing of the United States for starting the war. Instead, the treaty let the United States keep the territories of the Indigenous First Nation it had acquired and effectively left it free to continue spreading west.

According to an article by the Office of the Historian on the U.S. Department of State's website, the actual causes are varied but are evident in the treaty that ended the war, the Treaty of Ghent:

> *On Christmas Eve British and American negotiators signed the Treaty of Ghent, restoring the political boundaries on the North American continent to the status quo ante bellum, establishing a boundary commission to resolve further territorial disputes, and creating peace with Indian nations on the frontier. As the Ghent negotiations suggested, the real causes of the war of 1812, were not merely commerce and neutral rights, but also western expansion, relations with American Indians, and territorial control of North America.*

The treaty was signed on December 24, 1814, bringing a close to the War of 1812. After signing the treaty, Clay briefly traveled to London, where he helped Gallatin negotiate a commercial agreement with Britain.

After three years of fighting, the War of 1812 was officially over. Unfortunately, it took a while for the news to reach America, and battles and skirmishes continued. The news of overwhelming victory at New Orleans and of the treaty were spread at roughly the same moment, leading most of the United States to mistakenly believe that Andrew Jackson was the true hero of the War of 1812.

## OTHER OUTCOMES

While most history teachers are vocal about minimizing the War of 1812, there are two clear outcomes from all this loss and chaos and lots of small ones that warrant recognition. In so many ways, the War of 1812 changed the course of the United States and Kentucky.

1. Great Britain and all of Europe recognized the United States as the leader and independent country it was and began working with the United States as an ally, a relationship that continues today.
2. Perhaps most satisfying to the Kentuckians who had lost family members, health and limbs to the War of 1812 was that with the

death of Tecumseh and the defeat of the Pan-Indian Confederacy, the threats of Indian raids declined. More and more Indian tribes acculturated, and shortly after the end of the war, the remaining members of the confederacy opposed to acculturation moved beyond the Mississippi River. Never again were Indians able to band together meaningfully to oppose White settlement in the United States.

Some historians have called the War of 1812 not the Second War of Independence but the War of American Expansionism. There is merit to those statements, as White Europeans continued to press westward in their insatiable quest for free land and a fresh start, now with less opposition. While the self-reliant common man rose to a zenith, the fate of the American Indian tribes of the frontier diminished. With the end of the War of 1812, the Native Americans could no longer count on Great Britain to shield them from the flood of White settlers headed west. Settlers came in droves by the Erie Canal or through the Cumberland Gap. The next seventy-five years saw a rapid decline in the Native Americans' way of life, even for those tribes like the Cherokee or Choctaw that tried to adapt to the White ways of living.

A new philosophy had taken root: manifest destiny. Manifest destiny was a cultural belief that American settlers were destined to expand across North America. Full of themselves from their success, Americans adopted three basic tenets:

1. The special virtues of the American people and their institutions;
2. The mission of the United States to redeem and remake the West in the image of the agrarian East; and
3. An irresistible destiny to accomplish this essential duty.

Though the War of 1812 is remembered inaccurately as a relatively minor conflict in the United States and Britain, it looms large for Canadians and Native Americans, who see it as a decisive turning point in their losing struggle to govern themselves. Seeds of sovereignty in Canada were sown in 1812. The war had a far-reaching impact on the United States, as the Treaty of Ghent ended decades of bitter partisan infighting in government and ushered in the so-called Era of Good Feelings.

The war also marked the demise of the Federalist Party, accused of being unpatriotic for its anti-war stance, and reinforced a tradition of Anglophobia that had begun during the Revolutionary War. Perhaps most importantly, the war's outcome boosted national self-confidence and encouraged the growing spirit of American expansionism that would shape policy for the United States for the better part of the nineteenth century.

## REMNANTS OF THE WAR OF 1812 ALL AROUND US

Hundreds of towns and counties throughout the United States bear the monikers of those who led, fought and died during the War of 1812. For example, Ghent, Kentucky, traces its beginnings back to 1809, but when Henry Clay visited the area in 1816, he suggested that the town be called Ghent in honor of the Treaty of Ghent, Belgium, which he helped negotiate. Minnesota, Ohio, New York and West Virginia also have Ghent towns.

It's not surprising that many counties, towns and places are named after the heroic Kentuckians; indeed, they are everywhere throughout the state, but other states honored them as well. Isaac Shelby has counties named for him in Kentucky, Alabama, Illinois, Indiana, Iowa, North Carolina and Texas. General John Adair has counties named for him in Kentucky, Iowa and Missouri. John Allen, killed at River Raisin, has counties named for him in Kentucky, Indiana and Ohio. Kentucky, Indiana, Illinois and Missouri named counties after Joseph Hamilton Daviess, killed at Tippecanoe, and Kentucky, Missouri and Iowa counties commemorate veteran and vice president Richard M. Johnson. Four other Indiana counties—Owen, Spencer, Warrick and Whitley—are also named for Kentucky veterans from the War of 1812.

This frieze of the Battle of the Thames, showing Richard Mentor Johnson attacking Tecumseh, is part of the dome of the Capitol rotunda in Washington, D.C. *Courtesy of Wikimedia.*

With the war over, Americans seized on the various successes of the army and navy and celebrated the fact that the relatively young United States had gone toe to toe with the most powerful military machine in the world, fighting it mainly to a draw. The notable victory scored by Andrew Jackson at the Battle of New Orleans, in addition to the multiple successes of America's greatest frigate, the USS *Constitution*, proved to be reason enough to promote the American image at home and abroad.

Andrew Jackson's popularity and subsequent election as president ushered in what is today known as the Era of the Common Man. American political demographics were shifting. Suffrage became more widespread as property requirements to vote were dropped by the states, resulting in a massive surge in the number of eligible voters.

Painters shifted to reflect American themes in their works. Generals and politicians fell by the wayside as subject matter in favor of the fur trader, horse trader, farmer—the everyday White men who made the machines of American politics turn.

And the academics were joining the movement. Oliver Wendell Holmes believed that Ralph Waldo Emerson's *The American Scholar* was the United States' intellectual Declaration of Independence. In it, Emerson urged Americans to look not to Europe for their models but to themselves and American landscapes for inspiration. Emerson's 1841 essay "On Self-Reliance" had a lasting impact on the American creed of the worth of hard work and one's own labor.

Emerson's pen and thinking were built on the evidence of American significance revealed by the heroic actions of Kentuckians in the War of 1812.

Through the years since the War of 1812, these sayings and idioms are heard in political slogans, advertising and everyday speech:

- War Hawks (still used today to describe angry people and those who clamor for war)
- "Remember the Raisin" (Kentucky war cry)
- "Tippecanoe and Tyler, too" (political slogan during Harrison/Tyler campaign)
- "If men were angels, no government would be necessary." — President James Madison
- "Show respect to all people, grovel to none." —Tecumseh
- "Peaceably if we can, forcibly if we must." —Henry Clay, as a War Hawk

- "Don't give up the ship." —Captain James Lawrence's dying admonition to Chesapeake sailors, which inspired Oliver Hazard Perry at Lake Erie
- "We have met the enemy and he is ours." —Commander Oliver Hazard Perry to William Henry Harrison on securing Lake Erie for the Americans

Chapter 11

# NOTABLE KENTUCKIANS
# IN THE WAR OF 1812

### JOHN ADAIR (1757-1840)

John Adair was accused and later exonerated as one of the insurgents promoting the Spanish Conspiracy with Aaron Burr, but his participation in the War of 1812 and subsequent defense of Kentucky's soldiers against General Andrew Jackson's charges of cowardice at the Battle of New Orleans restored his reputation. He returned to the statehouse in 1817, and Isaac Shelby—his commanding officer in the war, now serving a second term as governor— appointed him adjutant general of the state militia.

John Adair (1757–1840) was governor of Kentucky from 1820 to 1824. Nicola Marschall, artist. *Courtesy of Wikimedia.*

### WILLIAM ATHERTON (1793-1863)

Atherton mustered into the Kentucky Militia at age seventeen and fought in the Battle of the Thames. His journal narrative of his experiences provides a rare common soldier's perspective of the War of 1812, and as such, his account is considered to be a critical source for studying the conflict. It gives gruesome testimony to how adept the opposing forces were at bushfighting and Indigenous war customs he observed during captivity.

## BLAND BALLARD (1761–1853)

Ballard served as a scout in George Rogers Clark's 1780 expedition into the Ohio country, as a scout for Clark's 1786 Wabash campaign and at the battles of Fallen Timbers and Tippecanoe. He was wounded and taken prisoner at the Battle of Frenchtown but was among the group of prisoners who were transported into Canada and so escaped the River Raisin Massacre. Following the war, Ballard served as a delegate from Shelby County to the Kentucky general assembly in 1800, 1803 and 1805.

## WILLIAM T. BARRY (1784–1835)

Elected to the Kentucky House of Representatives in 1807, William T. Barry became a U.S. House of Representatives member in 1810, leaving to serve in the War of 1812. Barry won several elections, seating him in both the U.S. Senate and Kentucky Senate. During his time in the Kentucky Senate, Barry, one of the early public education advocates, wrote to former president James Madison seeking support for subsidizing public education across the state.

## JOHN B. BIBB (1789–1884)

Born in Virginia, John B. Bibb volunteered as a private for a Kentucky regiment and was promoted to major after the Battle of the Thames. After the war, Bibb practiced law in Logan County, served in the Kentucky House and Senate and developed a new strain of lettuce he called "limestone lettuce" around 1865. Not commercially available until the twentieth century, it was renamed Bibb lettuce in his honor. Bibb died in 1884 and is buried in the Frankfort Cemetery. His home still stands on Wapping Street in Frankfort.

## DANIEL BOONE (1734–1820)

A legend in his lifetime, Daniel Boone was an explorer and hunter whose exploits made him one of the most famous frontiersmen in American history. Boone explored west into Kentucky in the 1760s and 1770s and established the frontier outpost of Boonesborough, one of the first White settlements in Kentucky, in 1775. When the Kentucky territory became part of Virginia, Boone was named an officer in the Virginia militia and spent the next several years trailblazing and fighting Indians. At age seventy-eight, Boone volunteered for the militia but was denied due to age. Since the 1820s, several actors have portrayed Boone in various buckskin costumes, always with a coonskin cap, an item still sold in frontier museum gift shops memorializing the intrepid frontiersman. The most popular of these portrayals was by the actor Fess Parker in the TV series *Daniel Boone* from 1964–70. The real Boone thought coonskin caps were silly and impractical. Boone always wore a beaver or felt hat instead, with a wide brim for keeping out the sun and

Daniel Boone. Engraving by J.B. Longacre, after painting by C. Harding. 1835. *Courtesy of Library of Congress 2004671936.*

rain. Boone died near St. Louis in 1820 at age eighty-five and is now buried in the Frankfort Cemetery.

## JAMES BOWIE (1796–1836)

Born in what is now Simpson County, Kentucky, but raised in Louisiana, Bowie enlisted in the War of 1812 but too late to see combat. James and his brother Rezin P. Bowie joined the Second Division, Consolidated, a Louisiana unit. In January 1815, according to family records, the brothers were on their way to join Andrew Jackson in New Orleans when they were informed the war was over. According to the historical marker at the Alamo, Bowie's brother once described him as a "stout, rather raw-boned man, of six feet height, 180 pounds in weight." Bowie had an "open, frank disposition," but when insulted or challenged, his anger was terrible. Hero of the Alamo and designer of the Bowie knife, Bowie died at the Battle of the Alamo in San Antonio, Texas, on March 6, 1836.

## EPHRAIM M. BRANK (1791–1875)

Muhlenberg County native Ephraim M. Brank is renowned as the soldier who stood on Andrew Jackson's break built to hold back the British in New Orleans, picking off oncoming soldiers. Fellow soldiers reloaded and handed him primed guns, one after the other. A statute of him mid-shot stands in downtown Greenville, Kentucky. An unidentified British officer wrote an account in a Boston newspaper of a lone marksman dressed in linsey-woolsey who faced down the British one by one as they approached:

*We lost the battle; and to my mind, the Kentucky rifleman contributed more to our defeat than anything else; for while he remained in our sight our attention was drawn from our duties; and when, at last, he became enshrouded in the smoke, the work was complete; we were in utter confusion, and unable, in the extremity, to restore order sufficient to make any successful attack—the battle was lost.*

Known as a "crack shot," Ephraim Brank fought at the Battle of New Orleans. *Courtesy of the Greenville City Government.*

## GEORGE ROGERS CLARK (1752-1818)

Born in Albemarle County, Virginia, on November 19, 1752, George Rogers Clark grew up on the fringes of the American frontier, and his life and aspirations were intimately tied to westward expansion. Clark left behind a lasting legacy as "Conqueror of the Old Northwest," and his efforts helped to secure more and more territory for the fledgling American nation. However, Clark's accomplishments did not come with monetary benefits, and Virginia failed to reimburse him for expenditures incurred during the war until after the War of 1812. Sadly, he spent the last days of his life deeply in debt and actively evading creditors. He died at his sister's home, Locust Grove, outside Louisville, and is buried in Cave Hill Cemetery.

## WILLIAM CLARK (1770-1838)

Like many of his contemporaries, Clark was tutored at home in pre-statehood Kentucky, learning wilderness survival skills from his older brother George Rogers Clark. Embarrassed about his writing inconsistencies—he spelled "Sioux" twenty-seven different ways in his journals of the Lewis and Clark Expedition—he sought to have his journals corrected before publication.

Familiar with the territory due to his expeditions with Meriwether Lewis, Clark led several campaigns up the Mississippi River during the War of 1812. When the Missouri Territory was formed in 1813, Clark was appointed governor. William Clark died in St. Louis at age sixty-eight. Clark was initially buried at his nephew John O'Fallon's property, now known as O'Fallon Park. The funeral procession stretched for more than a mile, and cannons fired a military salute. In 1860, he and six family members were moved to Bellefontaine Cemetery. The monument that marks their graves was dedicated in 1904 on the centennial anniversary of the Louisiana Purchase.

## CAPTAIN ISAAC CUNNINGHAM (1754-1795)

Cunningham commanded a company of Kentucky Mounted Volunteer Militia from Clark and Bourbon Counties during the War of 1812. He served in the state legislature in 1816 and 1827. Isaac and his brother Robert brought bluegrass seed from Virginia and were among the first to cultivate bluegrass and use it as a crop in Kentucky. The brothers were also prominent in importing, breeding and raising shorthorn cattle and Thoroughbred horses. Isaac and his wife, Sarah Harness, are buried in Clark County.

## GEORGE GIVENS (1740–1825)

George Givens was born in Orange County, Virginia, in December 1740, shortly after his father, Samuel, died. He served as a lieutenant in Lord Dunmore's War against the Indians and later as a captain in the Revolutionary War. He moved his family to Lincoln County, Kentucky, about 1780, settling on a four-hundred-acre grant from Virginia for his war services. But his military service was far from over. He fought with George Rogers Clark and Benjamin Logan against the Shawnee and Wabash at River Raisin, and at age seventy-two, he volunteered to ride with Governor Shelby (his next-door neighbor) and fought at the Battle of the Thames. He died at his Lincoln County home in 1825.

## DR. CHRISTOPHER COLUMBUS GRAHAM (1784–1885)

The epitome of a Kentuckian with flair, Dr. C.C. Graham stands out. He began exploring the frontier with his father with the "Long Hunters," getting to know Boone, Whitley, Abraham Lincoln, Jefferson Davis, Darwin and just about anybody who was anybody in his 101-year-lifespan. He served in not only the War of 1812 but also the War for Mexican Independence in 1822, and he ferried Chief Black Hawk and his sons across the river during the Black Hawk War of 1832. An outspoken health advocate, he told anyone who would listen that the rich soils of Kentucky, abundant wildlife and resources were a ticket to indolence. At age ninety-three, Graham decided to take on Big Bone Lick excavations. According to an article written by Graham for the *Louisville Courier* in 1877 titled "The Mammoth's Graveyard," he and ten men found ten barrels of bones, teeth of mastodons and mammoths and buffalo skulls. With his customary modesty, Graham declared his collection the best in the nation. At 101, he could shoot the head off a turkey, without glasses, at fifty paces. A treasure trove of Kentucky history, Graham spent hours providing first-person insight to historian William Belknap Allen for his *History of Kentucky* in 1872.

## RICHARD MENTOR JOHNSON (1780–1850)

Richard M. Johnson was born into farm life in 1780 in Bryant's Station, Virginia, soon to be the Commonwealth of Kentucky. Like Henry Clay, a lifelong opponent, Johnson was elected to the state legislature at just twenty-three years old, one year younger than state law provided, then was elected to the U.S. House of Representatives from 1807 to 1819. The War of 1812 was the defining moment in Richard Johnson's life. Johnson was serving in the House of Representatives at the time, but it was not unusual for a member of Congress to leave his seat in the House to participate in combat. Heading north with Governor Shelby, Johnson fought at the Battle of the Thames, and while he is reputed to have killed Tecumseh, there is little clear evidence to support that claim. Nevertheless, with the help of a catchy slogan, Johnson was able to parlay the legend into the vice presidency of the United States.

Richard M. Johnson during his Congress years. Charles Fenderich, lithographer. Lehman & Duval, printer. 1837. *Courtesy of LOC 2003655039.*

The last years of his life were a mixture of depression and failure. On November 19, 1850, Richard Mentor Johnson suffered a fatal stroke and died. The hero of the Thames and former vice president was laid to rest at Frankfort Cemetery in Frankfort, Kentucky.

## MATTHEW HARRIS JOUETT (1788–1827)

Born in Mercer County in 1788, Jouett graduated from Transylvania University before studying law. Jouett served as a volunteer officer of the Twenty-Eighth Kentucky Infantry in the War of 1812 and was among the survivors of the River Raisin Massacre. The company payroll of $6,000 disappeared during the slaughter. Jouett restored the missing funds to the militia from his earnings as a master portrait painter. He also painted portraits of his fellow soldiers from memory, including Hart and Colonel Allen.

## Simon Kenton (1755-1836)

Born at Bull Run Mountains, Virginia, in 1771, Simon Kenton established himself as a frontiersman, soldier and businessman when, at the age of sixteen, thinking he had killed a man in a jealous rage (over the love of a girl), he fled into the wilderness of Kentucky, West Virginia and Ohio. Kenton took advantage of his role at the forefront of settlement by claiming huge amounts of land through so-called and widely accepted tomahawk improvements, made by chopping his initials or "mark" into large trees at the four corners of the land he desired. Kenton served in the War of 1812 as both a scout and leader of a militia group in the Battle of the Thames.

## John Littlejohn (1756-1836)

Widely known as the Guardian of the Declaration of Independence, John Littlejohn was born in England and immigrated to America in 1767. At age twenty, he became a Methodist preacher and rode circuits in Virginia and Maryland. During the War of 1812, Littlejohn was a sheriff and collector of internal revenue in Loudon County, Virginia. When the British advanced on Washington, D.C., in August 1814, President James Madison ordered that the National Archives be sent thirty-five miles away to Loudon County. Littlejohn helped hide these archives, so although much of Washington was burned, the documents were kept safe. Littlejohn moved to Kentucky in 1818 and lived in Louisville and Warren County before settling in Logan County, where he is buried in Russellville.

## Reverend Reuben Medley (1785-1853)

Born in Madison County, Virginia, Reverend Reuben Medley was converted at a camp meeting in 1807 and served as a private in the Third Regiment (Dickinson's) in Virginia during the war. In 1820, he came to Chaplin, Kentucky, where he served as a cabinetmaker and Methodist minister. He is listed in the book *Historic Nelson County* by Sarah B. Smith, written in 1971, as one of the early preachers of the Methodist church in Kentucky and in *The History of Methodism in Kentucky*, which states:

> *As a preacher, he was very superior—a man of some learning, of great research, and of constant application, while nature had blessed him with*

*that gift so rare—the power of oratory; for he was a natural orator. His library was sufficiently large to be a wonder in those days; nor did it lie neglected, but from it he brought forth things new and old, by which to explain and enforce the scriptures. In the doctrines of the Church he was well versed, and could present them, especially baptism, in a strong and pleasing manner; while at reproof, instruction and persuasion, he was equally happy.*

Medley, his wife and several family members are buried in the Old Methodist Cemetery in Chaplin.

## GENERAL JAMES SHELBY (1784-1848)

Son of Governor Isaac Shelby, James volunteered for the War of 1812 and participated in the first Fort Meigs siege and Dudley's Defeat. Initially thought to have been one of the nearly 200 slaughtered or 350 captured, he made it home after his escape. His home, Richland, just outside Lexington, Kentucky, is currently under renovation.

Richland, the home built by James Shelby, son of Isaac, who was thought dead after Dudley's Defeat. *Author's collection.*

## JOHN SCOTT OAKLEY (1788-1845)

As a private in Captain Richard Menifee's unit, Donaldson's Cavalry, John S. Oakley fought alongside Colonel Johnson in the swamp and probably saw Tecumseh killed. After the war, he returned to Morgan County, Kentucky, where he farmed and was elected to the Kentucky House of Representatives in 1831—and he is the author's ancestor. He is buried on what was the Nickell Farm in Morgan County.

## ZACHARY TAYLOR (1784-1850)

Born in Virginia, Zachary Taylor's family moved to Louisville, Kentucky, when he was a boy. He served as a captain in the War of 1812 and became a national hero in the Mexican–American War, which led to his election as the twelfth president in 1849. Taylor died sixteen months later in Washington, D.C., and is buried on his family's homestead in Louisville.

## ROBERT SMITH TODD (1791-1849)

Lawyer, soldier, banker, businessman and politician Robert Smith Todd of Lexington fought at the Thames alongside Governor Shelby. He was also the father of First Lady Mary Todd Lincoln.

## DR. THOMAS WALKER (1715-1794)

Born in Walkerton, Virginia, Thomas Walker studied medicine and became a physician but was more interested in land speculation. He joined the Loyal Land Company and organized and led the first expedition through the gap in the mountains—which he named Cumberland Gap—in 1750. His expedition explored thousands of acres of land in the western wilderness of Kentucky decades before Lewis and Clark. Near the river—which he named the Cumberland—Walker built a cabin, widely accepted as the first house in Kentucky. A replica now stands on the part of the land claimed by Dr. Walker as a state historic site in Barbourville. He returned to his Virginia home shortly after that but left a journal documenting the hardships and discoveries of his travels and died at Castle Hill, Albemarle County, Virginia.

## WILLIAM CHAPMAN WHITLEY (1749–1813)

One of the first Kentucky pioneers in the days of Daniel Boone, William Whitley founded modern horse racing in the United States and made some of the first Kentucky sour mash whiskey. Some say Evan Williams and Jack Daniels still use his recipe. He built the first brick home west of the Allegheny Mountains, inlaying white bricks above the front door in the form of his initials, but his fame was that of an Indian fighter. At the advanced age of sixty-four, William Whitley volunteered to march to Canada in retribution for the River Raisin massacre and then volunteered to lead the Forlorn Hope to their deaths. His horse, Emperor, had one eye and two teeth shot out during the charge. The evidence is inconclusive, but eyewitness accounts point to Whitley as the man who killed Tecumseh. An account of Whitley killing Tecumseh and simultaneously being shot to death by the warrior was published in 1929 by his granddaughter.

The unusual brickwork of William Whitley's house had a large rendition of his initials inset over his front door. *Author's collection.*

## York (1770–1832?)

Born into slavery and enslaved by the family of William Clark in pre-statehood Kentucky, York participated in the Corps of Discovery Lewis and Clark Expedition from 1803 to 1806, where he proved to be a valuable explorer and member of that team. A slave owner known to deal harshly with his slaves, Clark brought York with him. The Indigenous nations treated York respectfully, and many Native Americans were interested in his appearance, which played a key role in diplomatic relations, according to journals. Other entries indicate that York was proficient in herbal medicine. Unfortunately, there is no clear record of what happened to York. Historians note that no documents conclusively establish that York was ever freed. Clark, however, in a conversation with the writer Washington Irving in 1832, claimed to have freed York. Many accounts have York dead before 1832, but there are also stories of a Black man, said to be York, living among Indians in the early 1830s.

*…and thousands more.*

# Chapter 12

# KENTUCKY TODAY

*I've seen the Northern Lights on the Yukon,*
*And the Southern Cross at the Equator.*
*But never have I seen anything to compare*
*With the soft shadows cast by the pale moonlight*
*Over the Bluegrass of old Kentucky.*
*—William Henson Dearen (1923–2004)*

As the thirty-seventh largest and the twenty-sixth most populous of the fifty United States, Kentucky has been known since colonial times for its politicians' writing and oratory, horse racing, bourbon distilleries, moonshine, coal, tobacco and bluegrass music.

It's known as the Bluegrass State, a nickname based on a species of grass found in many Central Kentucky pastures. It is said that early on spring and summer mornings when the fog is just beginning to dissipate and the sun has just risen over the horizon, if you look out across one of the horse pastures outside Lexington, Kentucky, there is just an impression of blue cast over the grass. But most of the time, the grass just looks green.

One of the main attractions for settlers to come over the Appalachian Mountains to Kentucky was its natural beauty. Kentucky honors this history with an expansive park system, which includes one national park, two national recreation areas, two national historic parks, two national forests, two national wildlife refuges, forty-five state parks (many of which commemorate battles, such as Blue Licks), 37,896 acres of state forest and eighty-two wildlife management areas. The Kentucky Parks system considers the fascinating geological features across the state and incorporates history and events from colonial days to the present day into parks development and programming.

## Kentucky Genealogy

Only Maryland, Delaware and West Virginia have higher German ancestry percentages than Kentucky, although most Kentucky first families trace their ancestry to the Scottish Americans, English Americans and Scots-Irish Americans who came to the state on land grants in the eighteenth century. These nationalities have heavily influenced Kentucky culture and are present in every part of the state through music, folk tales, literature and speech. Because the state was founded very early and settled quickly by soldiers and their families who stayed put for two centuries, intermarriage between immigrant families was common. After all, who else was there to marry but the sons and daughters of your neighbors? Because of this, it's common to hear genealogists relate, "If your family tree resembles a stick, you must be from Kentucky."

## Kentucky Creativity

From John Adair, Isaac Shelby and Henry Clay writing political speeches and essays to today's Kentucky authors, Kentucky has played a significant role in American and southern writing. Its writers produce works that detail their period and often celebrate the working class, rural life, nature and history and explore issues of class, extractive economy and family in the state's history. In recent years, several writers from Kentucky have published widely read and critically acclaimed books. These authors include Wendell Berry, Silas House, Barbara Kingsolver, Maurice Manning and Bobbie Ann Mason.

Kentucky today boasts two United States poets laureate, and both have been named to the office twice. Ada Limón was appointed United States poet laureate in 2022 for one year and again in 2023 for a two-year term, a first in U.S. poet laureate history. In addition, Robert Penn Warren (1905–1987) has the distinction of being both a U.S. consultant in poetry, 1944–1945, and the first person named U.S. poet laureate, 1986–1987, when the position was renamed.

And the Kentucky Music Highway leads travelers along a musical journey through a region steeped in storytelling and music. This scenic roadway rambles through seven counties in far eastern Kentucky, hugging the border of West Virginia and passing by some of Kentucky's most beautiful state parks and family homes of well-known musicians such as Loretta Lynn, Crystal Gayle, the Judds, Chris Stapleton, Billy Ray Cyrus, Tom T. Hall, Ricky Skaggs, Keith Whitley, Dwight Yoakam and Patty Loveless. Museums and music venues celebrating everything from bluegrass, country, ballads and folk music grew out of the heavy Scots-Irish influence in the region.

## KENTUCKY CULINARY TRAILS

From the first settlers who trekked Daniel Boone's Wilderness Trail through the mountains to the thousands of Appalachian Trail hikers today, the idea of trails has resonated with Kentuckians. And today, Kentucky seems awash with "trails" involving food or drink. To name a few: Bourbon Trail, Bourbon Craft Trail, Brewgrass Trail, Country Ham Trail, Fried Chicken Trail (which includes Colonel Sanders's original Corbin restaurant), BBQ Trail, Kentucky Donut Trail (curated by the *New York Times*), Sugar and Spice Trail in Newport, Bon Appetit Appalachia Trail and, of course, the Beer Cheese Trail.

Culinary trails may have started on the Kentucky River, where Johnnie Allman served his cousin Joe's Snappy Cheese at the historic Driftwood Inn. Today, the Beer Cheese Trail consists of thirteen stops (throw in the annual Beer Cheese Festival), each offering unique and delicious selections. No beer cheese in the world is more authentic than the kind made on the Beer Cheese Trail.

### Kentucky Beer Cheese

*1 bottle full-flavored beer*
*½ yellow onion, roughly chopped*
*2 teaspoons minced garlic*
*2 teaspoons Worcestershire sauce*
*½–1 teaspoon cayenne pepper*
*½ teaspoon salt*
*1-pound block sharp cheddar cheese*

At least 1 hour before making your dip, open the beer and let it sit on the counter. Add onion to a food processor and pulse until finely minced. Add all spices to the processor. Chop cheese into 2-inch cubes; add 1 cube to processor at a time while pulsing. Slowly pour in beer while pulsing until you reach a creamy consistency and no chunks of cheese remain. I usually use about ½ a bottle of beer or a little less. Serve with crackers, pretzels, carrots and celery sticks. Store leftovers in a tightly sealed container in the refrigerator.

Another ubiquitous Kentucky culinary delight, although a more recent invention, can be found at any restaurant in the state. It's the Brown Hotel's signature sandwich. In the roaring twenties, the Brown Hotel drew over 1,200 guests each evening for dinner and dancing. In the wee hours of the morning, guests grew hungry and moved on to the restaurant for a bite. Sensing their desire for something more glamorous than traditional ham and eggs, chef Fred Schmidt set out to create something new. His unique dish? An open-faced turkey sandwich with bacon and a delicate Mornay sauce. The Hot Brown was born! Today, iterations of the famous state sandwich can be found on nearly every menu in Kentucky. While there is no official Hot Brown Trail, Louisville has its own Hot Brown Hop, and websites tout an unofficial trail, frequently with spin-offs of the original. There are Hot Brown pizzas, Hot Brown omelets, veggie Hot Browns—just about everything you can imagine, usually using the traditional Mornay sauce. And most of them take care to stick to the flavors of the original. But the worst Hot Brown I've ever had used nacho cheese sauce. I don't recommend it!

Creating a Hot Brown at home sounds complicated, but it's pretty easy if you've ever made a roux. And all that cheese sauce… Mmmmm!

### Official Kentucky Hot Brown

*2 ounces whole butter*
*2 ounces all-purpose flour*
*8 ounces heavy cream*
*8 ounces whole milk*
*½ cup Pecorino Romano cheese, plus 1 tablespoon for garnish*
*Pinch ground nutmeg*
*Salt and pepper*
*14 ounces roasted turkey breast, sliced thick*

*4 slices toast (crust trimmed)*
*4 slices crispy bacon*
*2 Roma tomatoes, sliced in half*
*Parmesan cheese*
*Paprika*
*Parsley*

In a 2-quart saucepan, melt butter and slowly whisk in flour until combined, forming a thick paste (roux). Continue to cook the roux for 2 minutes over medium-low heat, stirring frequently to prevent scorching. Whisk heavy cream and whole milk into the roux and cook over medium heat until the cream begins to simmer—about 2–3 minutes. Remove sauce from heat and slowly whisk in Pecorino Romano cheese until the Mornay sauce is smooth. Add nutmeg, salt and pepper to taste.

For 2 Hot Browns, place 2 square slices of toast with the crusts cut off in each of 2 oven-safe individual dishes—cut in half corner to corner to make triangles—and place 2 triangle toast points per dish at opposite edges lengthwise. Then cover with 7 ounces of turkey and place sliced Roma tomatoes on top. Next, pour ½ of the Mornay sauce to completely cover the dish. Sprinkle with additional Pecorino Romano cheese. Place the entire dish under a broiler until the cheese begins to brown and bubble. Remove from broiler, cross 2 pieces of crispy bacon on top, sprinkle with paprika and parsley and serve immediately.

Established in 1999, the Bourbon Trail® is a road trip–style experience for bourbon lovers to visit the Bluegrass State's signature distilleries and learn its role in creating America's only national spirit: bourbon. In 2012, the Kentucky Distilleries Association (KDA) created the Kentucky Bourbon Trail Craft Tour® to complement the world-famous Kentucky Bourbon Trail® experience. The Kentucky Bourbon Trail® and the Kentucky Bourbon Trail Craft Tour® have drawn more than two and a half million visitors from all fifty states and twenty-five countries in the last five years. As a result, they have become leading educational and tourism attractions.

Last but certainly not least for the taste buds, western Kentucky is known for its regional style of barbecue that competes well with those of Memphis, North Carolina and other states. There is even a Western Kentucky BBQ Trail that showcases restaurants from Louisville to Paducah, each serving

After a devastating fire in 1996, Heaven Hill Distillery in Bardstown, Kentucky, built the Bourbon Heritage Center at the distillery. *Courtesy of Dixie Hibbs collection.*

up its own tasty (and, in several cases, award-winning) recipes. Or you could time a tasting trip with barbecue throwdowns like Fancy Farm Picnic or the International BBQ Festival for the feast of a lifetime—best washed down with a glass of strawberry lemonade.

## KENTUCKY HORSE RACING

Horse racing has been part of Kentucky's fabric since before it was a state. The clockwise track was invented here, and horse breeding is one of Kentucky's signature industries. Spring of every year brings Kentuckians and tourists from around the world to Kentucky to watch and bet on the races at the tracks, first at Keeneland in Lexington and then at Churchill Downs in Louisville.

But it is the first Saturday in May that captures the imagination and attention of people all over the world as they, in person or virtually, tune in for a weekend of horse racing unlike any other: the Kentucky Derby. Churchill Downs is one of the oldest Thoroughbred racetracks in the country and indisputably the most iconic. The famous twin spires on top of the grandstands are the most recognizable architectural feature in racing and are used as a symbol of the track and the Kentucky Derby alike.

Churchill Downs officially opened in 1875 and began its tradition as Home of the Kentucky Derby with two inaugural races, the Kentucky Derby and the Kentucky Oaks. Now, 149 years later, the Kentucky Derby is still going strong, making this the longest continually held sporting event in the United States. This race, for three-year-olds at one and a quarter miles, is the most famous race in the country and the prize most coveted by any horseman. Newborn colts are entered at birth, and trainers begin the onerous process to ready a colt to compete. Few of them make it. Preceded by an entire month of events like the Pegasus Parade, Thunder Over Louisville and more in Louisville and across the state, the Kentucky Derby helps to bring over $400 million to the Kentucky economy annually.

And across the globe, participants in fancy hats and outfits sip mint juleps, the signature cocktail for the race, whether in silver julep cups or paper cups.

### Official Kentucky Derby Mint Julep

*2 cups sugar*
*2 cups cold water*
*Sprigs of fresh mint*
*Crushed ice*
*Straight bourbon whiskey (like Old Forester Kentucky Bourbon Whiskey)*

Make a simple syrup by boiling sugar and water together for five minutes. Cool and place in a covered container with six or eight sprigs of fresh mint, then refrigerate overnight. Fill a julep cup with crushed ice, adding one tablespoon of mint syrup and two ounces of Old Forester Kentucky Whisky. Muddle a sprig of fresh mint into the glass. Sip.

The precursor to the esteemed race, the Kentucky Oaks, is for fillies and has its own signature cocktail, The Lily.

### Kentucky Oaks Lily Cocktail

*Crushed ice*
*1 ounce vodka*
*½ ounce orange liqueur*
*½ ounce fresh lemon juice*
*½ ounce simple syrup*
*3 ounces cranberry juice*
*Lemon wedges, for serving*
*Fresh blackberries, for serving*

Fill a collins or highball glass with crushed ice. Add vodka, orange liqueur, lemon juice, simple syrup and cranberry juice, then stir to combine. Garnish with a lemon wedge and a fresh blackberry. Enjoy!

Churchill Downs has recently undergone one of the most significant and ambitious series of reconstructions in its history. The construction of a turf course allowed the track to play host to the Breeders' Cup for the first time in 1988.

## KENTUCKY COLONEL

When the Kentucky Militia was deactivated following the War of 1812, Governor Isaac Shelby commissioned Charles Stewart Todd, one of his officers in the campaign, as an aide-de-camp on the governor's staff with the rank of colonel, and "Kentucky Colonels" was born. The title "Kentucky Colonel" was formalized in 1813, but early on, it was used informally to refer to people with honored reputations, often related to military service in the American Revolution. It was also often associated with landowners respected in their communities.

As the highest title of honor bestowed by the Commonwealth of Kentucky, commissions for Kentucky Colonels are given by the governor and the secretary of state to individuals in recognition of noteworthy accomplishments and outstanding service to a community, state or nation. An official certificate is issued to the bearer for display. Mine and my husband's are proudly displayed in our home, as were my parents' and as are my son's and daughter-in-law's in their homes.

In the late 1920s into the early 1930s, Kentucky Colonels began to come together to form a sociopolitical fraternal organization. Governor Ruby Laffoon founded the Honorable Order of Kentucky Colonels in 1932. Today, that organization funds arts and education programs across the state. In all, 190,000–310,000 Kentucky Colonels live in more than eighty-seven countries worldwide. It was initially a men-only club; the first woman Kentucky colonel, Annie Page, a newspaper editor from Ashland, Kentucky, was commissioned in 1920.

In 1936, New York advertising agency owner Colonel Arthur Kudner wrote a toast to Kentucky Colonels. The Honorable Order quickly adopted the toast, and it was widely published for use by Kentucky Colonels. The toast has since been ceremoniously presented at each of the Kentucky Colonels' Derby Eve Banquets:

*I give you a man dedicated to the good things of life, to the gentle, the heartfelt things, to good living, and to the kindly rites with which it is surrounded. In all the clash of a plangent world he holds firm to his ideal—a gracious existence in that country of content "where slower clocks strike happier hours." He stands in spirit on a tall-columned veranda, a hospitable glass in his hand, and he looks over the good and fertile earth, over ripening fields, over meadows of rippling bluegrass. The rounded note of a horn floats through the fragrant stillness. Afar, the sleek and shining flanks of a thoroughbred catch the bright sun. The broad door, open wide with welcome…the slow, soft-spoken word…the familiar step of friendship… all of this is his life and it is good. He brings fair judgment to sterner things. He is proud in the traditions of his country, in ways that are settled and true. In a trying world darkened by hate and misunderstanding, he is a symbol of those virtues in which men find gallant faith and of the good men might distill from life. Here he stands, then. In the finest sense, an epicure…a patriot…a man. Gentlemen, I give you, the Kentucky Colonel.*

# KENTUCKY BOURBON

One of the top finer things in life a Kentucky Colonel would be dedicated to would be bourbon. More than eleven million barrels of bourbon are estimated to be curing at any one time in Kentucky's rickhouses, squarish buildings that dot the roadside throughout central Kentucky in which bourbon barrels are placed to age. It is widely accepted that Kentucky produces more than 95 percent of the bourbon made in the world, leading to the belief that Kentucky has more barrels of bourbon than people.

In 1964, legislation declaring bourbon "a distinctive product of the United States" surfaced in Congress. In order for whiskey to be bourbon, it must be made with a minimum of 51 percent corn; aged in new, charred oak containers; stored at no more than 125 proof; and bottled at no less than 80 proof. Some lawmakers questioned giving special recognition to this humble, blue-collar drink, and their reluctance was easy to understand. Distilling was one of the most corrupt industries in American history. Prohibition had created a vast underground crime industry and linked bourbon to organized crime, an unintended side effect of Prohibition. But such a resolution provided trade protection against foreign competitors (like France does for champagne and cognac and Mexico for tequila). Staffers responsible for shepherding the legislation through Congress came to see it

*Above*: This realistic mockup of a still that might have been found at any time during the last two hundred years in Kentucky is set up in the Oscar Getz Whiskey History Museum. *Author's collection.*

*Left*: Henry Clay has had his name co-opted for whiskey and bourbon bottles at a variety of distilleries over the last two centuries. *Courtesy of Ashland, the Henry Clay Estate, Lexington, Kentucky.*

as a bit of a joke, assigning it to a handler who didn't know anything about the liquor trade but was named August Bourbon—the coincidence was too good to pass up. Nevertheless, the resolution passed, and America now has its own native spirit to promote.

And promote they have. Each year, the Bourbon Trails garner more tourists than any other single attraction in the state. Bardstown, Kentucky, is trademarked as the Bourbon Capital of the World. That distinction has led to a new bourbon theme park being built just outside Bardstown. Kentucky Owl Park, a collaborative venture with Beaumont Inn owner and Stoli Vodka based in Luxembourg, is a 420-acre site boasting five beautiful lakes with crystal clear, limestone-filtered water used in the production of Kentucky bourbons in the on-site distillery. Other internationally known distilleries—Maker's Mark, Heaven Hill and Jim Beam, to name a few—infuse Bardstown with history and spirits.

Only in Kentucky.

## AUTHOR'S NOTES

At least eleven of my Scots-Irish sixth-great-grandfathers on my mother's side received land grants in what is now Morgan County, Kentucky—for service as colonial scouts, guides and soldiers. My complete (both sides) Ancestry DNA test indicates that 90 percent of my genetic material comes from England, Ireland, Wales, Scotland and northwestern Europe; 2 percent from Norway; and the rest from Germanic Europe.

At present, I have two confirmed War of 1812 veterans in my family, John Scott Oakley and John Benjamin Perry, both from what is now Morgan County, Kentucky. I'm sure there are more, as eleven families I am related to moved to the area on Revolutionary War land warrants in the 1780s, founding what is now West Liberty. And that's just my mother's side.

I am a member of First Families of Kentucky, Transylvania Chapter of the Daughters of the American Revolution and the Kentucky Daughters of the War of 1812. There are many more lineage societies I qualify for, but these are the areas of historical interest for me.

If you have an ancestor who fought in the War of 1812, I encourage you to join the National Society United States Daughters of 1812 or the General Society of the War of 1812, no matter where you live. Registrars and members of these lineage societies would love to help you document your ancestry. Many Kentucky Revolutionary War veterans received more land as a result of service in the War of 1812 and moved farther west to Missouri, Texas, Oklahoma, etc. It is important to document history, and there were so many Kentuckians involved in this war that many have been lost to time. Let's remember them. Contact https://usdaughters1812.org (ladies) or https://gswar1812.org (men) for more information.

# SOURCES AND FURTHER READING

Allen, C. Leonard, and Richard T. Hughes. *Discovering Our Roots: The Ancestry of the Churches of Christ*. Abilene, TX: Abilene Christian University Press, 1988.

Bockstruck, Lloyd DeWitt. *Revolutionary War Bounty Land Grants*. Baltimore, MD: Genealogical Publishing, 1998.

Brown, Kenneth O. *Holy Ground: A Study of the American Camp Meeting*. New York: Garland Publishing, 1992.

Clark, Thomas Dionysius. *A History of Kentucky*. Ashland, KY: Jesse Stuart Foundation, 1992.

Clift, G. Glenn. *Remember the Raisin!: Kentucky and Kentuckians in the Battles and Massacre at Frenchtown, Michigan Territory, in the War of 1812*. Reprinted as two volumes in one with notes on Kentucky Veterans of the War of 1812. Baltimore MD: for Clearfield by Genealogical Publishing, 2002.

Collins, Lewis. *Collins' Historical Sketches of Kentucky*. Collins, 1877. Accessed on Google Books.

———. *History of Kentucky Volumes 1 and 2*. Collins, 1882. Accessed on Google Books. January 15, 2023.

Collins, Robert F. *Dragging Canoe*. By Patricia Bernard Ezzell (Tennessee Valley Authority). Tennessee Encyclopedia. Accessed on Google Books.

Cozzens, Peter. *Tecumseh and the Prophet: The Shawnee Brothers Who Defied a Nation*. New York: S.L., Vintage, 2021.

Eaton, Clement. *Henry Clay and the Art of American Politics*. Boston: Little, Brown, 1957.

Eckert, Allan W. *A Sorrow in Our Heart: The Life of Tecumseh*. New York: Bantam, 1993.

Ehle, John. *Trails of Tears: The Rise and Fall of the Cherokee Nation.* New York: Anchor Books, 1988.

Graves, Dianne. *In the Midst of Alarms.* Montreal: Robin Brass Studio, 2012.

Hammack, James W., Jr. *Kentucky and the Second American Revolution.* Lexington: University Press of Kentucky, 2021.

Harrison, Lowell H. *Kentucky's Governors.* Lexington: University Press of Kentucky, 2021.

Harrison, Lowell H., and James C. Klotter. *A New History of Kentucky.* Lexington: University Press of Kentucky, 1997.

Heidler, David S., and Jeanne T. Heidler. *Henry Clay.* New York: Random House, 2010.

Hibbs, Dixie, and Doris Dearen Settles. *Prohibition in Bardstown: Bourbon, Bootlegging and Saloons.* Charleston, SC: The History Press, 2016.

Hickey, Donald R. *The War of 1812: A Forgotten Conflict.* Urbana: University of Illinois Press, 2012.

Isenberg, Nancy. *Fallen Founder: The Life of Aaron Burr.* New York: Penguin, 2008.

Johnson, E. Polk. *A History of Kentucky and Kentuckians: The Leaders and Representative Men in Commerce, Industry and Modern Activities.* Chicago: Lewis Publishing, 1912.

Johnston, A.C., and E.S. Schweig. "The Enigma of the New Madrid Earthquakes of 1811–1812." *Annual Review of Earth and Planetary Sciences* 24 (1996): 339–84. Available on SAO/NASA Astrophysics Data System (ADS).

Kleber, John E. *The Kentucky Encyclopedia.* Lexington: University Press of Kentucky, 2014.

Klotter, James C. *Henry Clay: The Man Who Would Be President.* New York: Oxford University Press, 2018.

———. *Our Kentucky.* Lexington: University Press of Kentucky, 1992.

Leavey, Peggy Dymond. *Laura Secord: Heroine of the War of 1812.* 1st ed. Toronto: Dundurn Press, 2012.

Nash, Gary B. *The Unknown American Revolution: The Unruly Birth of Democracy and the Struggle to Create America.* New York: Penguin, 2006.

Pears, Thomas C. "Presbyterians and American Freedom." *Journal of the Presbyterian Historical Society (1943–1961)* 29, no. 2 (1951): 77–95. http://www.jstor.org/stable/23324687.

Redford, A.H. *The History of Methodism in Kentucky.* Ann Arbor: Michigan Publishing, 2006.

Schmidt, Leigh Eric. *Holy Fairs: Scottish Communions and American Revivals in the Early Modern Period.* Princeton, NJ: Princeton University Press, 1989.

Smith, Sarah. *Historic Nelson County.* Baltimore: Gateway Press, 1971.

Wrobel, Sylvia, and George Grider. *Isaac Shelby: Kentucky's First Governor and Hero of Three Wars.* Danville, KY: Cumberland Press, 1974.

Young, Bennet H. *Battle of the Thames.* Louisville, KY: Filson Club, 1903.

# Online Resources

Archer, Richard. "Dissent and Peace Negotiations at Ghent." *American Studies* 18, no. 2 (1977): 5–16. https://journals.ku.edu/amsj/article/view/2285.

Atherton, William. *Suffering and Defeat of the Northwest Army.* Frankfort, KY: 1842. Hathi Trust Digital Library. https://babel.hathitrust.org/cgi/pt?id=nyp.33433081804878.

Daughters of 1812. "Daughters of 1812 Society." https://usdaughters1812.org/.

Dos Passos, John. "The Conspiracy and Trial of Aaron Burr." *American Heritage* 17, no. 2 (February 1966). www.americanheritage.com/conspiracy-and-trial-aaron-burr.

Eslinger, Ellen. "Farming on the Kentucky Frontier." *Register of the Kentucky Historical Society* 107, no. 1 (2009): 3–32. https://www.jstor.org/stable/23387135.

Harris, James Russell. "Kentuckians in the War of 1812: A Note on Numbers, Losses, and Sources." *Register of the Kentucky Historical Society* 82, no. 3 (1984): 277–86. https://www.jstor.org/stable/23380342.

Historical Marker Database. https://www.hmdb.org/.

Iannacci, Nicandro. "Henry Clay: The Great Compromisor." National Constitution Center. https://constitutioncenter.org/blog/henry-clay-the-great-compromiser.

"Kentucky County." http://virginiaplaces.org/vacount/kentuckycounty.html.

Kentucky Guard. "Kentucky Guard Celebrates 229th Birthday." https://ky.ng.mil/News/Article/2670563/kentucky-guard-celebrates-229th-birthday/

Kentucky National Guard. "KY National Guard History the War of 1812." 2019. kynghistory.ky.gov/Our-History/History-of-the-Guard/Pages/The-War-of-1812.aspx.

Klein, Christopher. "How Enslaved Men Who Fought for the British Were Promised Freedom." History.com. https://www.history.com/news/the-ex-slaves-who-fought-with-the-british.

Lewis, James E., Jr. "The Burr Conspiracy." *American Heritage*. George Washington Prize Issue, 2018. https://www.americanheritage.com/burr-conspiracy.

Sprague, Stuart. "The Death of Tecumseh and Rise of Rumpsey Dumpsey: The Making of a Vice President." *Filson Club Quarterly* 59, no. 4 (1985): 455–61. https://scholarworks.moreheadstate.edu/cgi/viewcontent.cgi?article=1156&context=msu_faculty_research.

Tim Talbott. "First Race Course." ExploreKYHistory. https://explorekyhistory.ky.gov/items/show/321.

———. "Traveler's Rest." ExploreKYHistory. https://explorekyhistory.ky.gov/items/show/579.

Wikipedia. "List of Memorials to Tecumseh." https://en.wikipedia.org/wiki/List_of_memorials_to_Tecumseh.

# INDEX

## A

Adair, John 117, 123, 126
Adams, Abigail 86
Ashland 56, 57, 69, 145
Atherton, William 91, 126

## B

Bacon, Lydia B. 88
Barry, William T. 117, 127
Bibb, John B. 127
Blackfish 17, 19, 20
Bluegrass State 138
Boone, Daniel 20, 22, 23, 28, 30, 39, 50, 127, 128
Boone, Jemima 32
bourbon 47, 144, 146
Bourbon Iron Works 44
Bowie, James 128
Brank, Ephraim M. 129
Brock, Isaac 74, 77, 84

Brown, Dr. Samuel 43
Bubbleland 42
Burgoyne Cannon 114, 115
Burr, Aaron 59, 60, 61, 126

## C

Calhoun, John 65, 66, 67, 68
Chief Dragging Canoe 28, 30
Chief Roundhead 75, 77, 78, 81, 95, 97
Clark, George Rogers 19, 20, 37, 127, 130, 131
Clark, William 130, 137
Clay, Green 78
Clay, Henry 55–69, 120, 123, 124, 132
culinary trails 140–143
Cumberland Gap 18, 28, 29, 33, 37, 38, 122, 135
Cunningham, Isaac 130
Custer, George Armstrong 100, 101

# D

Donaldson, John 116
Dudley's Defeat 12, 53, 78–80, 102, 104, 115, 134

# F

Forlorn Hope 81, 112, 113, 136
Fort Detroit 77, 89, 109
Fort Meigs 12, 26, 53, 78, 79, 80, 87, 97, 102, 103, 104, 109, 115, 134
Frenchtown 53, 80, 94, 95, 96, 97, 99, 101, 109, 113, 115, 127

# G

Graham, Dr. Christopher Columbus 131

# H

Hampton, Wade 13, 118
hardtack 91, 93
Harrison, William Henry 12, 53, 75, 78, 83, 99, 102, 107, 109, 125
Harrod, James 20, 28

# J

Jackson, Andrew 44, 54, 118, 121, 124, 126, 128, 129
Jefferson, Thomas 36, 52, 60

Johnson, James 112
Johnson, Richard Mentor 53, 81, 111, 112, 114, 117, 123, 132
Jouett, Matthew Harris 51, 132

# K

Kenton, Simon 20, 30, 81, 133
Kentucky Colonels 145
Kentucky Derby 143, 144
Kentucky long rifle 31
King's Mountain, Battle of 49, 50

# L

Lincoln, Abraham 32, 47, 69, 84
Littlejohn, John 133
Logan, Benjamin 38, 131
Lord Dunsmore's War 49

# M

Madison, James 11, 12, 14, 47, 52, 62, 66, 72, 77, 124, 127, 133
Medley, Reuben 133
Militia Pig 107, 108, 109, 116
Monroviatown 54

# N

New Madrid 40–43
New Orleans, Battle of 14, 26, 44, 67, 86, 118, 121, 124, 126, 129

# O

Oakley, John Scott  117, 135, 148

# P

Pan-Indian Confederacy  25, 43,
54, 73, 76, 78, 122
Perry, Oliver Hazard  12, 13, 106,
109, 125
Prophetstown  73, 75

# R

River Raisin, Battle of  12, 13, 26,
54, 78, 80, 84, 87, 91, 92, 95,
97, 99, 100, 101, 102, 104,
113, 115, 123, 127, 131, 132,
136

# S

Second Awakening, the  22–23
Secord, Laura  89, 90
Shelby, Isaac  13, 25, 38, 39, 48–54,
78, 90, 104, 123, 126, 145
Shelby, James  78, 134
Sibley, Sarah Whipple Sproat  89
soldier slaves  85–86

# T

Taylor, Zachary  135
Tecumseh  12, 13, 25, 43, 70–84,
105, 107, 110, 111, 113, 114,
115, 122, 123, 124, 132, 135,
136
Tecumseh's Curse  83, 84
Tenskwatawa  25, 70–84
Thames, Battle of the  13, 26, 30,
54, 80, 105, 107, 113, 114,
117, 119, 123, 126, 127, 131,
132, 133
Tippecanoe  11, 73, 75, 76, 83, 89,
123, 127
Todd, Robert Smith  135
Treaty of Ghent  14, 15, 26, 68,
117, 118, 119–124

# W

Walker, Thomas  28, 135
War Hawks  26, 56, 62, 64–66, 124
Whitley, William  30, 81, 112, 113,
136
Wilderness Trail  18, 52, 140
Wiley, Jenny  33
Wilkinson, James  13, 39, 117
Williams, Samuel Luttrell  101

# ABOUT THE AUTHOR

oris Settles began researching her family history at thirteen years of age. As a lifelong Kentuckian begat from six generations of lifelong Kentuckians, that's a lot of Kentucky history to learn and celebrate. Even as a child, she devoured history books, interviewed anyone who would stand still, signed on for folklore classes in college and just generally collected bits of exciting information that happened her way.

Sitting on the front porch of her grandmother's house on North Third Street in Bardstown, Kentucky, peeling peaches or snapping beans, she listened to stories and questioned her grandparents and anyone who sauntered by. And she fell in love with the tales they told.

Fortunately, writing gave her an outlet. Her bylines have appeared in magazines such as *Working Woman, Family Circle* and *Kentucky Monthly*, academic journals and newspapers such as the *Kentucky Standard, Springfield Sun, Courier-Journal* and *Lexington Herald-Leader*. She has published two books on technology culture and taught writing at Lexington Community College (now Bluegrass Community and Technical College) and the University of Kentucky. Her academic background includes literature, journalism and instructional design.

Her interest in history prompted her to coauthor *Prohibition in Bardstown: Bourbon, Bootlegging and Saloons* with friend and native Bardstonian Dixie Hibbs.

In 2022, Settles published a children's picture book about gardening and an interactive garden journal for kids. That same grandmother encouraged her lifelong passion for gardening, and she volunteers as a Fayette County Extension Master Gardener.

Settles is a member of First Families of Kentucky, River Raisin Chapter of Daughters of the War of 1812 and Transylvania Chapter of the Kentucky Society of the Daughters of the American Revolution. She lives in Lexington, Kentucky, with her husband (another sixth-generation Kentuckian) and two very spoiled rescue pups.